WHIPPETS: REARING AND RACING

WHIPPETS:
Rearing and Racing

Pauline Wilson

FABER & FABER
London   Boston

First published in 1979
by Faber and Faber Limited
3 Queen Square London WC1
Printed in Great Britain by
Latimer Trend & Company Ltd Plymouth

British Library Cataloguing in Publication Data

Wilson, Pauline
  Whippets.
  1. Dog racing   2. Whippets
  I. Title
  798′.8   SF439.5

  ISBN 0–571–11320–6

Contents

Plates

9

Plates

Preface

It is over eighty years since a book was written solely upon the sport of whippet racing and, during that time, a transformation has occurred in the sport, although most people imagine these little dogs still run to their cloth-capped owners amidst a background of gambling and drinking!

Although this book mentions whippet racing in the old days, its main object is to show how the sport has progressed, how meetings are conducted, and how the present 'racing' strain has evolved. Purebred whippet racing also enjoys great popularity and a section has been devoted to pedigree events.

Help in writing this book has been very kindly given from various quarters, notably from Mrs. Hilda Meek, who researched the pedigree section; Mr. Ian Macdonald, without whose efforts the rag racing section would have been very difficult to compose; and Mr. Roy Green who supplied information on Blue Peter; additional help came from Mr. Sam Ernest, Mr. Jeremy O'Byrne, Mr. Jack Cadman and Mr. P. R. Sweeney. My sincere thanks to all these people for their kind help and encouragement.

PAULINE WILSON

Chapter One

EARLY DAYS

If any animal conjures up feelings of nostalgia, curiosity, enigma, it is the whippet, recognised by newcomers to the breed as being a 'scaled-down version of the greyhound'.

Always associated with the working class—especially the mining fraternity—the whippet, or snap dog (so nicknamed because he can catch quickly and snap at his game), has surpassed many of his canine colleagues in that the dog is still carrying out the work for which it was originally bred, i.e. racing and coursing.

Although some mystery surrounds the origin of the whippet, it is generally accepted that it is a cross between the greyhound (for speed) and the terrier, bull terrier, etc. (for gameness and intelligence). Rough-coated dogs were a common sight in the old days when the look of the animal was secondary to performance; however, it was soon realised that the smooth coat was more compatible with racing.

Even as long ago as 1850 whippets were seen in the mining districts of the North. Mill workers in the Lancashire area also boasted these minuscule racers, which at that time weighed as little as 7 lb. In those days the whippet was also used in the 'sport' of rabbit coursing, where a rabbit was enclosed in strange surroundings, chased by the dog and inevitably killed. This practice aroused a fair amount of criticism at the time and was banned after the turn of the century.

13

The whippet was accepted by the Kennel Club in 1890, and Darlington was the first Show to introduce a class for the breed under the title of 'snap dogs'. The year 1897 saw the breed first exhibited at Crufts, and the whippet was well and truly established! Not many breeds of dog are acceptable in so great a variety of colours as the whippet, which comes in fawn, brindle, black, blue, white, particolour or a mixture of the aforementioned.

NINETEENTH-CENTURY RACING

Whippet racing was popular in the latter half of the nineteenth century and the earliest book on the sport—*The Whippet and Race Dog*—was written in 1894 by Freeman Lloyd of the National Whippet Racing Club. At that time the sport had grown considerably and was taken very seriously indeed by owners, who went to any amount of time and trouble to present their charges in tiptop condition for a particular event. Indeed, it is a fact that in days gone by the whippet was held in high regard by a family, being really well looked after, even to the tune of sharing the children's bed! When times were hard this racer was often the only source of income and so had to be kept in peak condition.

BIG DAY OUT

In the late 1800s a visit to a whippet meeting was a big affair, being more of a spectator sport than it now is, probably due to the presence of bookmakers in those days. Several rings were roped off, apparently for the 'better class'; space was made available for carriages, which were charged by the wheel, a typical fee for a four-wheeler being 10s, while two-wheelers had to pay 5s; the 'public' also had their allotted standing points. In addition, amusements and refreshments usually accompanied this important event.

Lots of planning and work were involved in a whippet meeting of this type, for not only had the spectators to be taken care of, but the track had to be prepared: cinder tracks, rolled to bowling-green smoothness, were the order of the day; dogs raced to rag in string lanes and these had to be set out, and the weighing enclosure, paddock, etc. had to be roped off.

There were no such things as whippet traps: dogs were held by the scruff of the neck and the base of the tail and literally thrown from their respective marks. It is said that a slipper who could throw a whippet a good distance, with the animal landing on its feet and in its stride, was worth his weight in gold! Because of the human element in this method of starting, a special judge had to be appointed to see that, when the starting pistol was fired, all dogs were released together. And woe betide any slipper who was not up to scratch, as warnings given on some early whippet programmes state: '(1) Any dog slipped before the pistol is fired, slipper suspended till next meeting; (2) All slippers to toe mark when slipping; (3) Dogs slipped before the pistol, race to be re-run and neutral slipper to slip dog that starts before pistol is fired.' It was also an offence to slip a dog too slowly, which was sometimes tried in order to cheat the bookies!

TWENTIETH-CENTURY RACING

Interest in whippet racing continued into the 1900s; the workers of this particular period jealously guarded this form of relaxation, for what better tonic was there after a hard shift deep underground than to take to the fields with one's snap dog? What better way of escape from the everyday routine than a trip to the local to socialise with one's colleagues and weigh up the possibilities for a forthcoming meeting? What better enjoyment than when the big day finally arrives—the excitement of the racing, a flutter on a few fancies? And so whippet racing continued to thrive.

In the early 1900s one of the notable racers was a 21 lb. fawn dog, Comedian, who notched up many outstanding wins from 1903 right up to 1907, finding success at Fobney Grounds, Reading; Marsh Grounds, High Wycombe; Braywick Grounds,

Maidenhead; Pond House Grounds, Reading and North Berkshire Grounds, Abingdon. Another handy whippet of that time was Actor, who earned acclaim in 1904 and 1905 at the Cambridge Park venue of the Guernsey Whippet Club, being the first winner of a two-guinea gold medal.

National newspapers of the time reported whippet events; for instance, on 31 July 1910, at Manor Park Grounds, Messrs. Green and Crabb decided their weekly £3 5s 171-yard handicap. The result was a win for Wild Irishman, 12½ lb., second Young Admiral, third Togo.

The north-east, of course, was steeped in whippet racing and there was some good money to be won by the top racers of the day. As far back as 1919 at the Hendon Running Grounds, Sunderland, a £40 whippet handicap took place. Thirty-seven heats were run and the winner scooped £31, with other finalists sharing the remaining £9. Imaginative names such as White Rat, Bluff, Holey Rock, Pallion Lady, Whiting Pot and Dirty Dick were on this club's books.

Also, the sport has always been strong in Lancashire. After the First World War, one of the important clubs in the area was the North-East Lancashire Club at Stanhill, Oswaldtwistle. (This small Lancashire town still boasts a whippet club, now named the East Lancashire W.R.C.) Racing at this time was really popular and it was not unknown for entries of 300, meaning over thirty nine-dog heats! Cash was paid to the winners, so some good pickings were to be had.

On 1 June 1929, an open handicap was staged by the North-East Lancashire Club at the Athletic Ground, Stanhill, when dogs ran in twenty-four eight-dog heats over 200 yards for prize money as follows: Winner £5 10s, second £1, third and fourth 10s each, with heat winners not in the final each receiving 5s. Some of the dogs participating in this meeting were Bold and Bad (Nelson), Ugly Doll (Blackburn), Beat the Book (Oswaldtwistle), Never Heed (Blackburn), Rabbit Catcher (Bootle), Sore Eyes (Blackburn), Young Pinwheel (Blackpool) and Black Pudding (Bury) but the winner was a fawn bitch, Saucy Sue, from Blackburn, second Shamrock from Haslingdon, third Greta from Cambridge, fourth Mary from Blackburn.

There were many flourishing clubs in the 1920s, another of them being the Eastern Counties Whippet Racing Association, whose committee insisted that all dogs were registered, giving details of breeding, weight, sex, colour, etc. The Joker from Ipswich was a member of this Association, and also had some good wins at Portsmouth until being involved in a car accident.

A well-known haunt of West Riding owners and spectators alike was the cinder track at the rear of the Old House at Home public house in Bradford, the scene of many an hour's good sport. Still in the West Riding, the Airedale track used to boast electric judges even as far back as the 1920s.

Another 'strong' whippet area in the 1920s (as indeed it still is) was around Rotherham. In 1927, 150 yards straight racing took place on a cinder track at Low Ground, Rotherham, when dogs were hand-slipped to rag. As many as 200 spectators attended, with large entries and challenge matches weekly for as much as £20 a side. Two of the best dogs were Peggy, a 14-lb. white and brindle bitch, and Hamer, a 22-lb. fawn dog whose wins were considerable. In 1929 a set of traps was acquired, and dogs then chased a rabbit skin, winched up the track by a bicycle wheel. A charge of 1d entry to the ground was made.

The early thirties at Mexborough, Yorkshire saw twelve-dog races. Pedigree was not important, whippets and terriers competing side by side. This was a round track, to ball hare, dogs being released from traps. Winners at this club were 14-lb. Lucky and 16-lb. Tuppence, both dark fawn with black muzzles.

Yes, there was certainly plenty of activity in the whippet racing world—Cornwall, Stoke, the Black Country, Nottinghamshire, Lancashire, Yorkshire, Co. Durham, and Northumberland—throughout England these little dogs were providing many hours of entertainment for their fanatical owners!

Chapter Two

REBIRTH OF WHIPPET RACING

The Second World War put an end to virtually all organised whippet racing but, towards the end of the war years, enthusiasts in the north-east managed to resume their pastime. In 1941, a club was formed at Ellington near Morpeth, Northumberland, where only two dogs were raced at a time and racing was handi-capped by the dogs' height, i.e. 4 yards to the inch. Although a few dogs were over 21 inches, most were well under.

Eventually, interest was rekindled and the sport snowballed during the 1940s in the north-east: Newbiggin by Sea started its sweep in October 1945; Netherton in August 1945, Newsham commenced in May 1946 and Ashington in October 1949 (3 yards to the inch). Sometimes, dogs had to race as many as six times to win the handicap over 180 yards, two dogs at a time.

POTTERIES RACING

Whippet racing is very strong in the Potteries area and several clubs now enjoy success, but one of the first on the scene was the Stoke-on-Trent W.R.C. which was formed on 4 July 1948. Racing was in lanes to the rag, with up to eight dogs in each heat. There was no weight limit, but most dogs would be in the 25 lb. to 35 lb. bracket. After having been initially weighed-in, the handicap winner carried a 2-yard penalty, while heat winners retained their mark and others went forward half a yard. So popular was whippet racing at Stoke in the early days that between 80 and 100 dogs could be expected at each meeting, the crowd averaging 300. Eight to ten bookmakers were in attendance also, and the law allowed eight meetings a year in one field, hence the club had to move around the district.

Prize money of about £8 to £10 could be picked up at Stoke and all for an entry fee of 1s 6d per dog with programmes 6d or 1s. Racing took place on Tuesday and Saturday evenings.

A typical account for a meeting in the late forties is as follows:

INCOME	£	*s*	*d*	*EXPENSES*	£	*s*	*d*
Gate	15	11	9	Judge	1	0	0
Programmes	3	16	3	Starter		15	0
Dogs	5	18	0	Starter's assistant		15	0
Seven bookmakers	7	0	0	Handicapper		10	0
				Barker (calling dogs			
				to traps)		10	0
				Police		16	0
				300 programmes	2	5	0
				Prize money	8	0	0
				Sentinel advertisement			
				(local paper)		9	0
	£32	6	0		£15	0	0

THE NORTH-WEST

Organised whippet racing was revived in the north-west in 1955 when a small group of fanciers formed the Furness Club at Barrow-in-Furness. Racing was from traps up a stringed or netted lane to rag, five dogs per race. The majority of north-west whippets were descended from the oldtime Staffordshire strain.

By 1963 other clubs had formed in the north-west: Lancaster, Whitehaven, Dalton, South Cumberland and Ulverston. Five clubs had licensed tracks, complete with floodlighting for night

19

racing. During the summer it was possible to attend racing every weekday in that area.

THE SPORT SNOWBALLS

The Lancashire W.R.C. began racing in 1957, events being in string lanes, formed by wooden stumps and white elastic tapes placed one foot from the ground. Dogs had to be registered as to markings on limbs and body, date of birth, sex and colour of eyes.

The year 1958 saw the start of the Derwent W.R.C. at Dipton, Co. Durham, where a height limit of 21 inches was in operation and dogs were required to be 'genuine whippets', passing a panel of judges. Four-dog heats were held over 140 yards from hand-operated traps to drag hare. Club champion in the early days was Mick the Miller, clocking 8·95 for 140 yards.

The Sedgebrook W.R.C., Grantham, was a strong club in its day; formed in 1961, the weight limit was 28 lb., dogs racing 150 yards or 220 yards from traps to dummy hare. Eight yards was the maximum start in this Linconshire club's handicap.

Also formed in 1961 was the Little John W.R.C. which raced at Fishpool, Nottinghamshire. Six-dog racing was the order of the day over 185 yards to dummy hare and a 'dogs muzzled' rule was in operation. This club started off with a 30-lb. limit but this was subsequently dropped to 28 lb.

Birmingham was the 'mother' club of its district, but after it was formed members came from such a wide area that it was decided to save travelling by forming the Cannock West and Cannock Mid. Racing was over 105 yards and the track record was 6½ seconds (30-lb. limit). This area hand-slipped down lanes to rag. Still in Staffordshire, the Brierley Hill W.R.C. was founded in 1962 as a rag racing club up tapes. Notable racers of the time were Miss Deal, Dusty, C.B.S. and Fair Deal. From a small beginning, this club built up into a strong concern.

One of the most famous of the Yorkshire clubs of the 1960s—Kirkheaton W.R.C., Huddersfield—had a faltering start in that the inaugural meeting on Boxing Day 1962 had to be called off owing to bad weather. But eventually it enjoyed a very successful existence until it folded in the early 1970s.

At Southend-on-Sea, Essex, the Braeswood W.R.C. came into being in 1962; racing was from hand-operated traps to dummy hare, handicapped on time in eight groups. Fastest dogs were Pearlie Girl, Kitty Hawk, Arrowsmith and Black Arrow. Braeswood has stood the test of time and still flourishes.

Another club which has been in existence since 1962 is the Preston W.R.C. in the north-west. In its younger days, there was a 20-inch limit and many members also belonged to the Northern Counties Whippet Club, their dogs having appeared on many a show bench. Nowadays Preston W.R.C. alternates between bends and straight racing, and is an extremely popular club.

The Stockport W.R.C. came into existence in 1962, as an overspill from the Lancashire W.R.C. Dogs ran from electrically operated traps over 140 yards to rag.

The year 1962 also saw the start of the Lemington W.R.C., Newcastle-upon-Tyne, racing at Westerhope and known locally as the 'Royal Ascot'.

A 26-lb limit was in force at the Worcester W.R.C. which began meetings at Perdiswell in 1962 over a five-lane 130-yard track to rag.

Equipment-wise, the New Mills W.R.C., Cheshire (formed in 1963) was better than many, boasting electrically operated traps and a public address system. Events were over 120 yards, handicapped at 2 feet per pound.

And so whippet racing has captured the imagination of countless people who enjoy all that whippet racing has to offer. The sport has spread to all corners of England; Wales has a number of clubs; the Isle of Wight has its whippet club and racing is spreading far north into Scotland. What is so unique about whippet racing? I would say the opportunity of owning lovable and very game pets and, by one's own time and efforts, turning these same pets into open or club winners, while making a whole new circle of friends into the bargain!

21

Chapter Three

THE CHANGING FACE OF
WHIPPET RACING

Think of whippet racing and the old cliché 'cloth cap and muffler' immediately springs to many people's minds but, if any sport has been transformed, then whippet racing certainly has! No more is whippet racing a thing to be enjoyed by the head of the family alone; gone are the days when the sport was staged mainly for the punters' pleasure—one rarely sees a bookmaker in attendance at whippet meetings nowadays; gone also are many of the characters associated with the sport, such as the 'slipper' and the 'starter' whose pistol sent the slippers into action.

One thing that has not been lost as whippet racing has progressed is the enthusiasm of the owners. Although almost all organised 'rag racing' is now extinct, it is still quite a sight to see the four or five owners walking up the track after having secured their charges in the traps. Encouragement from these keen whippeteers takes many forms, but it is mainly in waving rags of many shapes and sizes, dog coats or the inevitable onion bag; vocal chords are also exercised in the hope that the animal will distinguish his particular owner's voice or whistle and so put in that extra burst!

Although still strictly an amateur sport, whippet racing has changed a good deal and become more organized. In place of the 'slipper'—once an integral part of the sport—are starting traps; the familiar sight of 'raggers' and the spectacular leap on to the rag at the finish by these canine athletes is now a rare sight as, with very few exceptions, the dogs chase a dummy hare. This in itself brought with it another change, that of muzzling the runners. When dogs ran to rag, obviously mouths needed to be unhampered in order to catch hold of the rag, but the change-over to 'lure' racing brought with it the controversy that dogs should be muzzled to safeguard the racers as all contenders converged on to one lure. Eventually the good sense of muzzles was accepted and only isolated meetings do not call for dogs to be muzzled, as well as the rag clubs of course.

There is now much more communication between whippet racers in all parts of the country. In the past, whippet clubs had to rely upon the local and national press to publicise forthcoming events but now the sport has its own magazine which covers whippet racing nationally.

The British Whippet Racing Association has played a major part in promoting friendship between enthusiasts hailing from all corners of Great Britain. Their two major Championship meetings have become regular opportunities to renew old acquaintanceships, and the increase in open meetings ensures that whippet owners are constantly making new friends.

The most striking change in whippet racing is that it is ever increasingly a 'family' sport. More and more wives and children now take an interest and one sees almost as many women as men at whippet events. The popularity of whippeteering amongst children is self-evident as countless youngsters own, train and race their whippets. It is an ideal sport for children to undertake for, with a little adult guidance, a young person can obtain hours of pleasure from his or her dog, looking after the animal, walking the dog with good purpose in mind and, on race days, experiencing the thrill of winning or sometimes the disappointments which accompany any competitive sport.

Whippet racing is now a pastime which is enjoyed by men, women and children in all walks of life and more and more are taking up the challenge these game little dogs offer!

Chapter Four

CLUB RACING

Wherever a whippet-owner lives in England—especially in the Midlands and North—there is almost certain to be a whippet racing club in the vicinity.

Owing to the noise problem in built-up areas (barking dogs and Sunday afternoon naps are not compatible and therefore clubs are often the subject of complaints by local residents!) whippet clubs are only too pleased to avail themselves of any piece of land offered, and whippet racing may take place on football fields, rugby grounds or disused aerodromes. Local councils are often helpful in finding racing venues. Social clubs, miners' welfare clubs, etc., are particularly sympathetic about making ground available for whippet racing and it is generally found that whippet clubs based on miners' welfare grounds have excellent facilities, good equipment and the blessing of the welfare committee.

Joining a whippet club is usually a simple matter; just pay the annual membership fee and you're in, although in the case of whippet clubs on welfare grounds, an owner may also be obliged to join the 'mother' club.

Racing is held on Saturday or Sunday, with many clubs operating midweek racing during summer: only a couple of clubs can boast floodlighting, so winter evening racing is out.

RACING PROCEDURE

Straight racing always takes place on grass tracks which may vary from 140 to 200 yards in length. Dogs are released from wooden or (more commonly) metal traps similar but, of course, smaller than greyhound starting boxes. These are commonly hand-operated, but may also be electrically operated by energising solenoids.

The incentive nowadays, since the demise of rag racing, is a 'lure' i.e. a rag which is clearly distinguishable. A common 'lure' is an onion bag, not because of the scent (whippets race by sight, not smell), but purely because these are brightly coloured and of an open weave which prevents excessive mud collecting on them in adverse weather conditions, and can easily be kept clean, yet remain lightweight, simply by dipping them in a bucket of water from time to time. Onion bags are also easily acquired, and owners can obtain them from their local greengrocer for home training.

The lure is propelled along by a machine which can take many forms. One of the first methods used (and still used occasionally) was constructed out of a bicycle frame and a tyreless rear wheel, the cord wrapping around the wheel rim. Other forms of hand lures consist of many improvisations from pieces of gear wheels and pulleys; even sheep-shearing machines have been converted!

The more popular method nowadays (bearing in mind the lack of mains electricity at most clubs) is a 12-volt car starter motor mounted on a suitable frame and fitted with a pulley, powered by a 12-volt battery. Speed usually is regulated by depressing a circuit breaker according to the speed of the dogs. More sophisticated equipment is fitted with variable rheostats. Most lures are made by enterprising club members, but commercially made traps and lures are available.

Some clubs are fortunate enough to own electric timing equipment, but generally a manual stopwatch is used, an experienced timekeeper being able to perform this operation competently.

Judging also relies on the human element (a handful of clubs own photo-finish equipment); two judges are necessary, one on either side of the finishing line, and a unanimous decision is required for a dog to qualify. In the event of a split decision, it is declared a dead-heat and may be re-run. The starter judge stands fairly close to the front of the traps and is responsible for checking that muzzles are correctly fitted before he declares the race ready to proceed. Another judge stands halfway down the track, his duty being to watch for any interference in the race.

Club racing may be run on one of a few methods of handicapping but, whichever is used, it should be so designed that all dogs eventually have the chance of a win, otherwise the same few dogs would take the prizes week after week.

HANDICAPPING ON WEIGHT

This is the simplest form of handicapping (and many say simplest is best) and would seem to eliminate the chances of cheating. When taking part in the handicap for the first time, a dog is weighed (usually on spring-balance scales, the dog safely supported by a specially made weighing harness) to determine his handicap mark. One yard per pound handicapping is popular (although half a yard per pound is not unknown), therefore a dog concedes or receives the same number of yards as he weighs heavier or lighter than his opponents, i.e. a 20-lb. whippet would have 5 yards' start from a 25-lb. dog, but would have to give start of 2 yards to an 18-pounder.

After the handicap is over, the dogs' performances determine the marks for the following week; winners will move back in the handicap, while losers either stay on the same mark or move up a yard according to the method operated by the club and, this way, all dogs eventually find their own level. The first few weeks of a new handicap are dominated by the faster dogs, who then waste no time in rapidly working their way to the back, supposedly handicapping themselves out of it and giving the slower dogs a chance.

HANDICAPPING ON TIME

By far the most common approach to handicapping whippets (also used in greyhound racing) is the time method whereby a dog is given a trial run up the full distance and his mark is decided according to the time clocked. The handicap may be worked out at 0·07 seconds to the yard, but more usually at 0·06 seconds to the yard; this may sound complicated, but actually means that with, say, a scratch time of 9·10 seconds for 150 yards, a dog clocking 9·40 would race off 5 yards. This is arrived at by dividing the difference between the time set by the scratch dog (9·10 in this instance) and the time clocked by the trialling dog (9·40). The difference in this case is 0·30 (0·06 into 0·30 equals 5 yards). In cases where the figures do not divide exactly, this is taken to the nearest yard, viz. a dog doing 9·43 would race off 5, but a time of 9·44 would mean a mark of 6 yards.

Time racing, in theory at least, means that all dogs should come over the line in a 'blanket' finish and very often they do, largely depending upon the skill of the handicapper. In the majority of cases, losing dogs move up the handicap system to enable them to find a winning mark eventually after which, of course, they are penalised.

Often a club also times heat winners and crossheat winners and a dog runs off its fastest time, i.e. if a dog does a faster time in a crossheat then it is penalised for this when running in the final. A slower time means the dog stays on the same mark. This method makes for closer racing.

MIXED BAG

There are clubs which do not operate on any one method of handicapping, but prefer to add a touch of variety to their racing. For instance, one week all dogs may race off scratch, another week yard per pound is the order of the day and time racing may also be fitted into the agenda.

For a whippet of fair talents, the club operating a mixture of handicaps may prove very palatable but, for the slower dog who needs to build up his yardage before being capable of winning, the regular 'time' or 'weight' handicap is much more suitable, otherwise it is highly possible that certain dogs will never have the sweet experience of crossing the line first!

GRADED RACING

Another popular method which seems to be very fair is 'grading', where dogs are grouped according to performance. This means that all dogs capable of clocking fast times will race together in the 'A' grade, with slower dogs being grouped in the 'B' grade, and even slower dogs making up the 'C' grade. Dogs may race off their weight mark within the respective groups, and if whippets are penalised for a win and therefore move into a higher grade when a certain standard is reached, then all dogs are given a fair crack of the whip by this means.

DISTANCES

For straight racing, distances vary somewhat, many clubs being governed by the land available. For safety reasons, an over-run of at least 25 yards at the finish is desirable and, at the starting end, room is needed for the trapman to work in comfort. In these circumstances, there are clubs which are left with a mere 140 yards' track distance, but this is quite sufficient, although an increased distance to, say, 150 up to 175 yards allows more scope, especially when it comes to hosting meetings on behalf of the two main bodies in whippet racing: the British Whippet Racing Association and the Whippet Club Racing Association.

BEND CLUBS

Bend racing is now becoming very popular both with pedigree and non-pedigree clubs. Many of the pedigree clubs are fortunate in being able to erect permanent bend tracks which are highly praised and very popular. One or two non-pedigree clubs are lucky enough to have ground available for permanent bends but most bend clubs are based at 'flapping' greyhound tracks or greyhound training kennels. Very few whippets will not go round the bend, indeed some take to it like ducks to water. Bend racing provides extra thrills for spectators as it is more unpredictable, and whippet racing on the bends is highly successful.

Bend handicapping can either be on time or weight (usually in weight groups) and whippets can have as many as three runs around the distance in any one meeting, as whippeteers usually want the satisfaction of finding a final class winner, as opposed to greyhound meetings where each race is an individual event. Bend distances can be anything from 220 yards up to 350 yards according to circumstances.

The stamina of these bend racers is remarkable: they are every bit as keen on the last run as on the first. Some whippets take to the bends so perfectly that, whereas they may be mediocre in straight racing, they are transformed when racing at a stadium, and earn great fame as 'bend' dogs.

BEATING THE HANDICAPPER

Whichever method of racing is used, there are a few who go all out to win by fair means or foul, in fact some people regard it as a real feather in their cap to 'beat the handicapper!' Weight racing leaves only one or two loopholes, i.e. a 'steadying' hand under a dog suspended in the weighing bag can successfully shed a pound or two! A more serious offence is to weigh in a 'ringer' that is, a

B   29

dog strongly resembling the runner, but one which weighs a pound or two lighter, thus gaining a few extra yards' start. Time racing, unfortunately, is more open to cheating, but with club 'advance and retard' systems, not much dishonesty occurs as it is pointless.

It is the big one-day time events where the tricks may be tried, for instance, old favourites like a tight muzzle-strap, a rubber band round the toe, chewing gum between the toes, with a hardened few stooping even lower! By means such as these, owners hope for a slower time trial, therefore a better mark!

While giving this warning, it is only fair to point out that, with the thousands of dogs running each week, the incidence of cheating is very small indeed.

Chapter Five

OPEN HANDICAP RACING

In sharp contrast to 'club' handicap racing which would seem to give all dogs the chance of winning sometime during the season, 'open' handicap racing is so designed that the superior dogs blatantly dominate the placings. Whippeteers do not seem to mind this; 'open' racing is regarded as a yardstick by which to measure one's own whippet. That certain dogs seem to pick up the prizes time and time again is of no consequence; whippet owners are an extremely optimistic breed, and nowhere is this more clearly illustrated than in open racing. A dog who displays talent on the open circuit commands great respect and is the subject of much admiration and envy.

An 'open' handicap is so named because, although usually staged by a whippet racing club, the meeting is open to all comers. Open meetings vary considerably as to the method of handicapping, distance, and so on, but one usual common denominator is that the great majority are run on a weight basis, i.e. all dogs are weighed-in at the commencement and handicapped accordingly.

Distances may vary from 140 to 200 yards for straight handicaps, increasing to as much as 300 yards for bend meetings. The most popular form of open handicapping is 1 yard per pound, i.e. the heaviest, or limit, dog would race off the scratch mark with others receiving a start of 1 yard for every pound weight less than the heavier dog, for example, a dog weighing 28 lb. would concede 5 yards to a 23-lb. whippet. In this method of racing, dogs would first be drawn into four- or five-dog heats; winners progress to crossheats, and victorious dogs in this section go on to race in semi-finals, which find the three or four dogs who are to contest the final.

Another common type of open is the 'weight class' event where all dogs within a certain weight division are grouped together. If racing was in 2-lb. weight classes, dogs would all race off scratch, but if the weight divisions were greater, say 4-lb. or 5-lb. classes, then dogs would be handicapped 1 yard per pound within classes. Normally, weight-class winners run-off to find a supreme champion for the day, but some clubs are satisfied to stick with just the division winners, one advantage of this being a wider distribution of prize money.

A more modern trend in open whippet racing is to segregate dogs and bitches, in effect to run two opens on the one day, one for dogs and one for bitches. It seems to be an established fact that a whippet bitch is faster than a whippet dog—there are exceptions of course—and this type of open has done much to enhance the popularity of dog whippets. In the days of purely integrated racing, the aptitude of many a good dog went by unnoticed as bitches really dominated the scene, but in segregated open racing the excellence of numerous top-class dog whippets really comes to light.

It is a fallacy that whippets will not race round a bend, in fact bend open meetings are extremely popular, distances varying according to the venue. Proprietors of greyhound stadiums have found that whippet racing really gives them a boost because, contrary to greyhound meetings where a programme of eight or so races are spread over an evening's allotted two or three hours, as many as 100-plus whippets can take part on any one day. Racing is either in weight classes off level breaks, or dogs may be handicapped $1\frac{1}{2}$ yards per pound, the extra half yard per pound being due to the extra running distance involved. The accompanying gate money, catering revenue, etc., makes these meetings for miniature racers good money spinners for small stadiums or 'flapping' tracks and consequently we have a boom in bend racing.

Entry fees for an open handicap vary from about 75p to £1.25 per dog, of which a percentage is paid in prize money and trophies. All dogs winning heats receive small prizes such as rosettes, medallions, trophies or perhaps a small cash prize. Dogs reaching finals receive cash in accordance with the number of entries; trophies may also be awarded.

No open handicap would be complete without the accompanying 'scratch' racing. This always captures the full attention of spectators, as the scratch dogs can always be relied upon to provide some cracking finishes. Scratch racing caters for dogs who, because of their weight, are prohibited from running in the open handicap proper and, whatever the weight of the dogs, all race from the scratch mark. Owners pay £1 to enter a dog in the scratch race and the winner either takes all or, in some cases, 10 per cent is deducted for club funds.

Different weight limits may be imposed on scratch racing, according to the traditions of the area and at many north-east clubs a 21-inch shoulder height replaces weight restrictions. In a few cases, no weight limit whatsoever is in operation, provided a dog is not a full greyhound—if the dog fits into the trap it gets to run! There have been some notable 'scratch' dogs over the years and, in fact, a good scratch dog can actually earn more prize money than an open handicap whippet.

One big misconception the public appears to have about open, or indeed club, whippet racing is regarding bookmakers. Bookmakers are in attendance at only a very few opens and this small number is on the decline. In days gone by when bookies attended opens, owners took the fullest advantage of the situation by entering dogs under false names to get better odds, thus turning the day into a farcical guessing game! Whippeteers now realise the foolishness of this anonymity and one seldom sees a name change at the rare open where bookies have been invited.

A modern trend in 'open' racing is the 'maiden' meeting which is open to dogs or bitches who have not previously won an open.

By this means, the really top dogs are barred from taking part, but these meetings still attract whippets of fair quality, so the 'club' whippet still has an impossible task to reach a final!

In view of the increasing popularity of open handicap racing, *Whippet News*—the national magazine covering the sport—runs a national competition in conjunction with open handicap racing, whereby dogs score points from open heat and final wins. This is run over twelve months, from January to December, the winning dog on points receiving a trophy, with coat badges and certificates going to the Top Ten dogs. Only genuine opens are taken into consideration, thus giving all dogs an equal chance, and any year's Top Ten generally reads like a *Who's Who* of racing whippets!

Although, with an above-average whippet, there is some reward to be earned on the open circuit, financial gain is not the incentive which compels whippet-owners to travel the length and breadth of the country to participate at open level. Travelling is expensive nowadays, as indeed is feeding and rearing dogs; even so, in this amateur sport, money is secondary to the prestige of owning and training a winner.

Chapter Six

RAG RACING

Although almost completely replaced by lure racing, ragging was at one time the only form of whippet racing.

DEFINITION

Rag racing is a term often used by whippeteers to differentiate this form of the sport from the now more popular lure racing, but the correct terminology is 'straight-lengthing', a phrase more accurately depicting its essence.

The object of a participant in any race is to go from start to finish quicker than the others, but the method of doing this and the type of route taken naturally vary with the nature of the event.

In lure racing, dogs chase a moving target along an open strip of land which may be straight, curved or even circular but in straight-lengthing they run to their trainers who have walked from them to the end of the track and who then attract them, normally by waving large cloths or rags. This track must be straight and divided into lanes, each lane being 3 to 4 feet wide.

Although whippets participating in a lure race are theoretically chasing the moving skin or onion bag, invariably their owners will urge them on vocally from the finishing end, some even waving rags. In straight-lengthing the ideal 'rag dog' makes a beeline for his master's rag, and those that do certainly make an exciting spectacle as they hurl themselves at their quarries. The important thing is that he has a clear run to do so, unimpeded by dogs that would take his ground or jostle him if it were not for the protection of his lane.

BASIC TRACK

These lanes may be defined in any of a number of ways. Over a 150-yard course, wooden stakes will normally be driven into the ground at intervals of 20 to 25 yards in a straight line, from the start to a point around 15 yards after the finishing line. A parallel line of stakes will then be established a yard or so to one side of this, and then further lines depending upon the number of lanes required—usually five or six. The simplest way of then completing the running track is to lay a length of string along each line, attached to each stake in turn, often by twisting around the stake. Ideally there should be two strings to each line; one at a height of around 15 inches to stop a dog jumping over, and the other at between 6 and 9 inches to discourage 'ducking under'.

Slight variations have been tried on this method to lessen the chores of setting up and taking down, but the most effective divider for a permanent track is coarse netting 18 inches or so high, although more stakes are required for this to take the weight. It is also advisable to use stakes which will stand around 2 feet from the ground in order to lessen the risk of injury to an inexperienced racer who might be tempted to cross lanes, or indeed to any dog which may slip.

TYPES OF COMPETITION

Straight-lengthing in the twenties and thirties must have been very similar to that practised forty years later. Gambling was a strong influence, and although the average racing dog was apparently smaller, he was nonetheless a practical breed, of the 'handsome is as handsome does' variety, with long-haired examples possibly even in the majority.

The *Sporting Chronicle* seems to have done a lot to promote the sport, and prize money that would top today's biggest offerings was raced for at the big events. Numbers involved must have been tremendous, and eight-lane tracks were required for the biggest events, to cater for the nationwide entries.

Handicapping in these events was usually based on the weights of the whippets although, perhaps surprisingly, a far more intelligent approach was made to the problem than can be seen practised by most organising bodies in open handicaps in recent years. These still insist on impractical rules of thumb such as 1 yard per pound, without any thought for the ratios involved or the distance raced. A typical 'run and weigh' scale of the period shows that there was no preference given to the 20- to 26-lb. weight group—both the 35-lb. and 15-lb. whippets were given a winning chance, assuming they were good enough. This scale was extremely well thought out with every quarter pound being taken into consideration.

THE POST-WAR REVIVAL

During the 1940s the whippet population dwindled, along with many other things, and only strongholds such as the Midlands and the north-east retained a strain. It was mostly the Staffordshire breed—easily recognisable through the broad chest, back and head of the Staffordshire bull terrier—that replenished stocks in the north-west in the 1950s.

At this time traps were not in common use and so, as of old, a skilful 'slipper' was of great value, the finer points of his throwing action when launching his charge down the track making the difference between a flying start and an undignified spreadeagle, the latter offering the dog no winning chance in a reasonably handicapped race.

Betting was still the main attraction, and as bookmaking was at this time not a licensed profession and the Customs and Excise Betting Duty Inspector non-existent, a high level of wagering was carried out, with perhaps a dozen bookmakers at each race meeting.

DUNGEON MEADOW, ROOSE, BARROW-IN-FURNESS.
(LICENSED 1957)

ELECTRIC JUDGE & DISPLAY

FLAG POLE

OFFICIALS' BOX

NOTICE BOARD

FLOODLIGHTS & POSTS (NOT TO SCALE)

PRACTICE LANE

SHRUB & MARSH LAND

TERRACING (RAILWAY SLEEPERS)

TRAPS

RAIL

FLOODLIGHTS FOR BOOKMAKERS

STARTER BOX

CAR PARK

REFRESHMENT HUT

BECK

BRIDGE (RAILWAY SLEEPERS)

ALLOTMENTS

HEDGE

EQUIPMENT STORAGE HUT

SHELTER

TOILETS

PROGRAMMES

ENTRANCE

LENGTH OF RUNNING TRACK: 140 YDS.

38

The Furness district of Lancashire probably took the sport to its highest level of sophistication. Formed in the mid-1950s, the Furness Whippet Racing Club built up a good following, racing on various fields until finally settling down at Dungeon Meadow, Roose, on the outskirts of Barrow.

A track was constructed there and granted a licence in 1957. This provided a permanent site for five-dog racing, utilising the latest electric traps, first-rate floodlighting and electric judge.

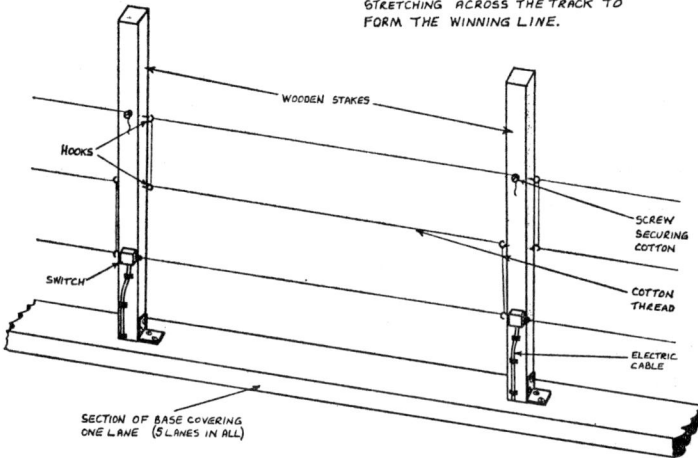

PART OF THE ELECTRIC JUDGE, STRETCHING ACROSS THE TRACK TO FORM THE WINNING LINE.

The judge was simple in principle; it was not foolproof, bus most important, it could be seen to be fair, as opposed to humant who might have a financial interest in the result of a race. It consisted of a set of spring-loaded magnetic switches—one per lane—each attached to a stake on the finishing line between lanes, the stakes being held rigid by a common base running across the track in a neat trench so as to be flush to the running surface. A length of cotton was attached to the moving contact of the switch and stretched back and forth between the lane's two stakes via four hooks at varying heights. It was pulled taut until the switch contact was fully opened, and was then fastened to a screw on one stake, thus holding the switch open until it was broken.

All five switches were connected through a 12-volt battery and set of electric relays to (in this case) five coloured lamps corresponding to the colours of the collars worn by the five runners. The winning dog broke his cotton first, closing his switch which, via the relays, simultaneously lit up his colour and cut out the other relays so that no other light came on, except in the case of a dead-heat.

A track offering basically similar facilities was licensed at nearby Dalton and another permanent track, but with mechanically operated traps, at Millom. Together with the unlicensed Ulverston Club, these tracks brought the sport to a saturation point for the keen gambling follower in 1962, with nine meetings each week during the summer, seven of which could be attended by the same person and each within a half-hour car ride or train journey. As only the licensed clubs had floodlights, this number dropped to six during the winter!

An idea of the number of whippets in training in the area at that time can be gauged by the fact that Furness-registered dogs were not allowed to run in the Dalton club and vice versa and that, although both clubs ran two meetings each week with sixty to eighty entries per meeting, no whippet could race twice even in the same club.

Extra opportunities to race came via the Ulverston and Millom clubs, which also had their own regulars, so during the summer of 1962 there must have been over 300 dogs running in well over 100 races each week.

This intense popularity had to wane eventually, and the Dalton club disbanded in 1964, only to be replaced within weeks by a new private venture which had been built during the summer at Ormsgill in Barrow. In addition to the features already mentioned, this track boasted a covered stand, bar and, most important of all, a photo-finish camera. This track enjoyed great success over the next few years, and a further saturation point was reached around 1966 when, with two nights' racing each week, the Thursday meeting attracted a regular ninety dogs. Interest dropped again, partly owing to the introduction of betting duty in

1966 until in 1969 the photo-finish was dropped and within two years the track was dead.

It was then up to the Furness club, which had lost out heavily to Ormsgill, as they were forced to race on the same nights, to pick up the pieces and for a few years both they and Ulverston kept ticking over, although interest was steadily diminishing.

The Furness track betting licence was relinquished at the end of 1974 and apart from a handful of occasions in 1976, there was no further gambling on the track, the few remaining members going through the weekly Thursday night ritual of setting out the gear, running a thirty-dog programme and putting the gear away again. A casual visitor might well have wondered why they bothered but to the members, many of whom had raced for years, it had become a conditioned action—Thursday night was whippet night, come what may.

TO FLAP OR NOT TO FLAP

Until the late sixties a track betting licence meant that a club could run about a hundred race meetings a year on a permanent site, but only on the two nights a week specified by the local authority. In Barrow, the Furness and Ormsgill tracks both had to race on Thursdays and Saturdays, whilst the Dalton club, coming under the Lancashire County Council, was allocated Mondays and Thursdays. Further up the coast Millom and Whitehaven took the Cumberland days of Monday and Saturday.

The varying fortunes of the sport over its twenty-year period of post-war revival in the north-west can be seen reflected in the progress of the Ulverston W.R.C. Taking its following from members of both Furness and Dalton, it remained unlicensed for many years, and was thereby able to pick its own race nights, usually Tuesdays and Fridays.

The disadvantage of not holding a licence was that the club was forced to 'flap' about from field to field, not more than eight race meetings being allowed in one year on the same site. This is the original meaning of the term 'flapping track'.

For a six-month season, six different temporary tracks had to be set up around the area embracing Ulverston, Askam and Dalton— not an easy task as it is almost impossible to find six flat fields on the fringe of south Lakeland, let alone obliging farmers with no use for them other than for grazing, and storage of equipment in these circumstances was quite a problem. But interest was high and coffers full, so difficulties were soon overcome. With the demise of the Dalton club in 1964, however, the Ulverston club licensed a field at Dalton and settled down to race on Mondays only for the next five years.

At a time when interest was flagging, however, and basic economics were governing the club's policies, the Lancashire County Council decided to double the annual licence fee to £100, and at this point the licence was given up and flapping resumed.

The year 1976 was survived by hiring the Furness track for a short 8-week summer season in order to allocate the annual trophies but, by the start of the next year, the officials had had enough and handed over all assets to the Furness club.

THE GOOD TIMES

The dogs racing at these north-west rag clubs varied greatly in size, although once the Furness club dropped its 21-inch limit in 1965 the bigger dogs predominated.

Handicapping was done basically in one of two ways. The Furness W.R.C. at its peak employed a handicapper who placed the whippets in their heats each week, allocating handicap marks (in units of half a yard) according to his assessment of their ability, based largely on the times they had put up. Only the lanes were drawn for. He would grade the dogs so that handicap starts of more than 4 yards were unusual, the slowest never competing against the fastest at graded meetings, and there were always sufficient entries for this to be done without the same whippets meeting too often. An owner would pay 1s to enter his charge, and the winner of each five-dog race would receive 30s or £2. On a normal night's racing, winners would not run-off in a final, the format of the programme being similar to that of a greyhound meeting, with ten to twelve races at 12-minute intervals.

In general, the other clubs, and later Furness also, adopted a more automatic racing system. The normal racing programme would consist of two handicaps, each composed of five or six heats of five or six runners per heat, and each being run-off to a final, one for the faster or 'first grade' whippets, and the other for the slower 'second grade' racers.

There would also be 'special' races, extra to the handicaps, for those over and above the numbers that could be accommodated in these handicaps. A typical method of varying a dog's handicap mark week by week was to give him a half-yard 'lift' every time he failed to win his heat, and to 'pull' him $1\frac{1}{2}$ yards if he won the final. It will be appreciated that as each runner has its own lane and therefore a free run, then a good genuine animal can be relied upon to reproduce its form faithfully and to clock surprisingly consistent times on a given track.

Allowances have to be made, of course, for overall fitness (in the case of a bitch, her calendar), and the characters of the various runners all play their part, but a more rewarding medium for the astute betting man, who does not mind taking the trouble to study available form, would be hard to find.

There was always a strong emphasis on the times clocked in rag racing, and track records were a popular talking point, as were scratch races.

Yard per pound racing was never practised in the Furness area's heyday, the highlights of the racing season being the invitation scratch races and matches, the holiday handicaps and occasional open handicap. In the last two instances, winners were always re-assessed round by round according to the times recorded.

Each track might hold just one, or maybe two, scratch races in a year so these took on a roughly similar role to horse racing's classics, as opposed to the programme-fillers one sees these days at club and open levels alike. One reason for the low number of scratch races must have been the fact that, with handicapping such a fine art, five or six of the fastest dogs running together off 'levels' presented too easy a task for the punter; so long as the fastest dog was also genuine, he was a 'cert', although the meeting of champions from the various clubs always created great rivalry.

HOLIDAY TIMES

Easter, Whitsuntide, August Bank Holiday and Christmas were special occasions, when the ordinary club races run during the week concerned served as elimination heats for the appropriate holiday handicap, the winners going through to the crossheats (semi-finals) and grand final, which would be run on the Bank Holiday.

The first breakthrough in the strained relationship between the Furness and Dalton clubs (officially attributed to the fact that the Dalton club was regarded by the Furness committee as being run as a private enterprise, profits going to Dalton Station Social Club), came with the introduction of open handicaps. There was one in the first year, two in the second and, as can be imagined, these were great occasions when reputations were put to the test, as many whippets had not raced before outside their own clubs, and many a Dalton owner relished the thought of a run on the hitherto forbidden sea-washed turf of the Furness club.

SOLITARY RAG CLUB

Only Furness now survives as a strictly rag racing club (Stoke W.R.C. stages rag and lure racing), a reminder of a time when all whippet racing was to the rag. Rag racing will probably continue here for some time yet, but in a form far removed from the exciting days of the late fifties and early sixties.

Chapter Seven

THE VARIOUS BODIES IN
NON-PEDIGREE WHIPPET RACING

BRITISH WHIPPET RACING ASSOCIATION

The B.W.R.A. was formed at a meeting held at the Golden Lion Hotel, Halifax, Yorkshire, on 3 June 1967, the aims of the Association being 'to promote greater friendship and understanding between the whippet racing clubs; to give strength to the advancement of the sport; to help clubs in dealings with local councils in negotiation for land, and to control and standardise whippet racing'.

Ten regions make up the B.W.R.A., i.e. Scotland, North-east, North Yorkshire and South Durham, Lancashire, South Yorkshire, East Midlands, West Midlands, Wales and Border Counties, Mid West and finally the South, each individual region having its own committee and running its affairs according to the rules of the Association. The executive committee presides over the periodical national committee meetings made up of representatives from all ten regions.

A member of a club which is affiliated to the B.W.R.A. is entitled to join the Association via his club secretary, and dogs must be registered with the B.W.R.A. before being eligible to participate in Association events. The national registrar keeps a record of all dogs registered, and the naming of dogs must be original, i.e. once a name has been selected and registered by an owner, it is his sole privilege to use that particular name in B.W.R.A. meetings. Membership cards and dog registration cards are issued and members are required to produce these when entering an Association event.

In its annual national race meetings, the B.W.R.A. tries to cater for all types of whippet, staging the Spring Classic time event, Puppy championships, Veterans' racing, inter-regional team events on both bend and straight, also a yearly rag racing championship when winners earn the title 'Rag Racing Champion'.

By far the most popular B.W.R.A. events are the bend and straight National Championships which are the highlights of the B.W.R.A. calendar. Each region stages 'qualifiers' where dogs and bitches run separately in 2-lb. weight divisions from 16 lb. up to 32 lb., the first and second whippets in each class going through to the National Finals three weeks later. By this method of elimination the best possible racing spectacle can be assured at the National Finals, when the very best from all regions assemble and spectators invariably witness a supreme display of racing from the cream of the country's whippets. Winners of each of the nine weight groups (dogs and bitches) attain the prefix 'Racing Champion' and it is for this reason that both bend and straight Championships are well supported.

No money is paid out in B.W.R.A. national race meetings, winners being rewarded with trophies of a high standard. If they desire, however, regions are allowed to pay prize money, and some are a hive of activity, putting on regional race meetings, open events, league racing, etc.

The B.W.R.A. National Secretary is Mr. A. W. Forrester, 12 Bonnard Close, Meir Park, Blythe Bridge, Stoke-on-Trent, Staffs. (Tel. Blythe Bridge 4324) to whom enquiries may be addressed.

NATIONAL WHIPPET RACING FEDERATION

The year 1976 saw the formation of the Federation by a group of people interested in promoting 'better organised open meetings, with better monetary rewards'. Its aim is to put more money into the sport, with membership and registration fees being ploughed back in the form of prize money. Federation meetings are held at the variety of affiliated club venues over different running distances and, besides races for top dogs, slowcoaches are also given the opportunity of racing for big prize money. Each Federation meeting carries a guarantee of a minimum of £100 prize money and trophies.

The Federation Secretary is Mr. G. K. Wigfield, 4 Cemetery Road, Hemingfield, Barnsley, Yorks. (Tel. Barnsley 754737).

LEAGUE RACING

In some areas league racing figures very prominently on the racing calendar, most of this being independent of the B.W.R.A. but run on a 'club team' basis. A league may comprise a number of clubs, and matches are held at regular intervals, points being accrued at each match to find the eventual 'League Champions'. These leagues are usually very efficiently organised with trophies and, in some cases, prize money being awarded to dogs gaining notable achievements in league events.

Chapter Eight

BREEDING AFTER THE WAR

Only a handful of pre-war racing whippet strains were left from which to breed and the Staffordshire strain was mainly responsible for today's racing whippets from such stud dogs as Lone Eagle, Swift Hawk, Oh Boy, Cracker and Bilko.

A 24-lb. whippet, Blue Smoke—All England Champion in the late 1940s—was mated to a Stoke bitch, Queenie, which produced Jackie, a leading sire of the 1950s. From Blue Smoke's mating to Black Elf came Saucy Sal who ran at the Stoke club. Saucy Sal was eventually mated to Joey—a Staffordshire dog—producing Shino (alias Swift Hawk) and Merrylegs. Another mating for Saucy Sal, this time to a sire named Sammy, gave Lone Eagle, well known as the sire of the outstanding stud dog Golden Link (out of Golden Lass).

Jackie mated many bitches, but the best offspring were Cracker (himself sire of Little Tipsy and Dido) and Golden Eagle (dam of March On). Other Jackie litters (out of Merrylegs) included Oh Boy, Kerry Girl and Satan.

Swift Hawk sired excellent stock, notably Bilko (out of a pedigree bitch), March On and WAP. Eventually, two notable sires emerged—Blue Peter and Bilko—and these two were mainly responsible for strengthening the racing whippet stock after the sport again took a firm hold in the 1960s. Their pedigrees are as follows:

```
                                                        Blue Smoke (L)
                                 Jackie (S)
                                                        Queenie (S)
                 Joker (S)
                                 White Girl (S)
                                                        Coyney Lass (S)
BLUE PETER (S)                   Blue Smoke (S)
                 Jean (S)                               Bobbie (S)
                                 Mellor's Rose (S)


                                 Joey (S)
                 Shino (S)
                 (alias Swift Hawk)                     Blue Smoke (L)
                                 Saucy Sal (S)
BILKO (S)                                               Black Elf (L)

                 Mossfield Margaret (S)
                 Pedigree
```

(S: Stoke   L: Leamington)

Blue Smoke, a 24-lb. dog owned by Mr. Harry Smith of Emscote, Leamington, Warwick (not to be confused with Blue Smoke from Stoke) was a flyer and he is fourth generation in both instances. In Blue Peter's pedigree it is the local Stoke dog Blue Smoke who is sire of Blue Peter's dam Jean.

A closer examination of Bilko's pedigree shows Shino as his sire; Shino was sold and renamed Swift Hawk. Digging still deeper into Bilko's pedigree, a bitch named Saucy Sal is unearthed, the dam of Lone Eagle who is found in the family tree of one of our present-day greats: R. Ch. Good as Gold. Actually, what has been excavated with this scrutiny of bloodlines is one basic and unarguable fact, that all the great racing whippets of yesterday, today and indeed tomorrow, can be traced back to Box Lane, Stoke-on-Trent in the late 1950s and early 1960s.

BILKO

Although this 28–30-lb. fawn dog was a very good club racer, he never found fame as a yard per pound dog, simply because there was not the opportunity at the time. Also, the dog was a very poor traveller. Bilko was owned by Mr. G. Bowers of Staffordshire whose colleague, Mr. Jack Scott, owned 35–40-lb. Gay Spot, who was quarter greyhound. Bilko and Gay Spot were mated, pups were sold for 30s and all the litter turned out to be winners, Spot On eventually being sold for £200. The next litter included Bang On, a name which speaks for itself.

Thus Bilko's name as a stud dog was established: the list of open racers bred by him is almost endless, and the modern racing whippet owes a lot to this famous sire.

Blue Peter

Bred by Mr. Bill Taylor of Stoke-on-Trent on 26 April 1959, Blue Peter was one of a litter of four, the others being Joker II, Fair Lady and Benny. His first owner kept him for only a matter of weeks, after which he was acquired by Mr. R. Aimison who owned him until he was bought for £10 in the early months of 1962 by Mr. Joe Mather of Stockport.

While under the ownership of Mr. R. Aimison, the dog was raced to the rag at a venue known as Box Lane, Stoke-on-Trent, competing against some of the fastest and biggest types of racing whippets in the country. The handicapping system was on time, and penalties for handicap final winners (pulled 3 yards) were harsh considering the fact that this penalty was carried by the dog for the rest of its racing life at this club. One consequence of such a handicapping system was that the club's best and most consistent dogs often changed hands simply because they had become out-handicapped.

When ownership had been transferred to Mr. Mather, Blue Peter was raced extensively at the Lancashire Whippet Racing Club in preference to Box Lane. Exact details are very hard to come by about Blue Peter's prowess as a racer, however, when he raced at Box Lane. There he was in the category of the good to moderate class of dog but it must be remembered that he was competing with whippets whose dimensions were comparable to those of small greyhounds. In this era of whippet racing it was at club level that enthusiasts sought competition, with entries of seventy to eighty being commonplace at Box Lane. The handicapping system, as previously stated, was on time (weight racing just simply would not be tolerated) with severe penalties imposed on the ultimate final winners. The competition was, without doubt, the toughest in the country, and bearing this fact in mind and the assurance that Blue Peter had won thirty-nine races at Box Lane, Joe Mather needed little else to convince him that he must own this dog.

With his acquisition of this blue dog, Joe Mather began to race him extensively at the Lancashire Whippet Racing Club (Agecroft) where he quickly enforced his dominance. In his first full season there he collected all but one of that club's trophies. A special feature of this club was to award certificates of merit to members' dogs for certain performances of distinction, and Blue Peter received numerous certificates duly signed and dated by the then club president Mr. Tom Hindle, a famous advocate of rag racing.

Blue Peter raced in various challenge matches during his career, some of the more notable opponents being Jacpin, Bilko, Our Kid and Candy, and during an inter-county match, Lancashire *v.* Cumberland, he ran against Consul. His career ended after taking 3 inches off his tail which caused him to retire from racing. Indisputably, Blue Peter's main claim to fame is that, during his long career at stud, he sired 1,042 puppies, amongst which have been a great number who were destined for open success. Following in his footsteps as notable stud dogs came Blue Fawn and Wishy Was, to name but two. Blue Peter is the only dog to have a whippet track named after him; in fact, the dog is buried on the site of the Stockport (Blue Peter) Whippet Racing Club in Cheshire.

Chapter Nine

SOME OF THE GREAT BROOD BITCHES

It is generally acknowledged that the bitch is mainly responsible for whether or not a litter turns out well. Every now and then a bitch comes along who turns out good pups time and time again, and these pups also usually find success in breeding.

BABY DOLL

Breeding Cheyenne Boy ex Lots Bluet of Elegance, this pedigree bitch was an outstanding racer in her day. Weighing 23 lb., she could compete with the best. Her matings to Blue Peter produced Dolly Blue, Blue Cloud, Right Royal, All The Blues, Sue and Blue Fawn, who himself turned out to be one of the country's top stud dogs.

SCARBACK

Mated to Bilko, her progeny included that incredible bitch Little Mary, also Cleo (the latter, when mated to Golden Link, produced the famous brother Good as Gold, now a stud dog, and sister Silver Dawn). Also out of Scarback was open winner Gay Boy and Robbo, sire of B.W.R.A. Supreme Champion Roberta D, a magnificent racing bitch who in turn was responsible for good consistent pups. One of these, Pendle Witch, has been seen to possess that extra something which denotes a good brood, as her pups have also found fame on the open circuit. So it goes on. Scarback was the dam of a line which can be depended upon for consistency.

GOLDEN WYN

First bred to Blue Fawn (Blue Peter ex Baby Doll) which brought that excellent fawn heavyweight Blackie; a mating to Darley Fly (Bilko ex Tearaway) saw an even better litter which included Cherry, one of the fastest lightweights ever, Kushi, who was also open class, and Della who proved a pretty good brood bitch herself. Another litter to Darley Fly produced Piper, then a change of sires to R. Ch. He's-a-Dandy saw What-a-Cheek and Hot Chip, good-quality stock.

CLOEY

A fast bitch in her racing days, she was mated to El Diablo (Bilko ex Alma) and the result was four dogs, namely Pedlar (B.W.R.A. Supreme Champion), R. Ch. Tinlegs, Bramble Star and Crazy Horse. Pedlar and Tinlegs were superior racers and all four found fame at stud. Cloey was exported, depriving the British whippet scene of perhaps bigger and even better things.

YOUNG LUCY

This black bitch was a whippet cross collie greyhound and, from her first mating to Bilko came Red Baron and Warlord, also the superlative bitch Little Lucy. The remainder of her matings were to Blue Fawn, offspring including R. Ch. Simo, R. Ch. Scrat, Three Blank, Lucy's Boy, Laverton Gold (dam of open runners), R. Ch. Cassandra. Of the dogs, only Red Baron has ever seriously taken up stud duties with much success.

GOODTURN

This Liverpool bitch was bred out of a greyhound, sired by pedigree dog Big Ben and was one of a very good litter (her sister being dam of Regal Kandy).

Although good on the track, R. Ch. Goodturn was better known as a brood bitch; out of her first mating to Right Royal (Blue Peter ex Baby Doll) came open winner She Sings, also some very fine club dogs; her next mating to R. Ch. Jim Lad gave Star Turn (open winner), R. Ch. My Turn, R. Sally and Jim's Star; a mating to R. Ch. Nip produced R. Ch. Hotspur. This line runs true to form, as She Sings' first litter to Wishy Was included top notchers R. Ch. Holly Lane and Sing On, twice B.W.R.A. Supreme Champion.

DAWN FLASH

This Lancashire bitch was renowned for always giving a high quality litter, both dogs and bitches. R. Ch. Dawn Star was one of her progeny (sired by Bilko) and three of her dogs were first rate on the track, Elio Flash, R. Ch. S.A.G. and Kaz-Garas, the latter two later having flourishing stud careers.

MAID MARION

Owned by Mr. and Mrs. D. Ashley of Nottinghamshire, this 26-lb. powerful bitch was one of the fastest whippets to race at the Little John W.R.C.

When mated to Bramble Star (El Diablo ex Cloey) the litter included three brood bitches, Julie's Maid, David's Maid and Rosalie's Maid. Julie's Maid was put to Kaz-Garas (Bilko ex Dawn Flash) and two first-rate bitches were to make their name on the track, i.e. Tracy's Maid (a black) and R. Ch. What-a-Maid (fawn). A mating to R. Ch. Nip produced the excellent bend dog Blackamoor, then a change of stud dogs to R. Ch. Good as Gold and the whippet world was talking about yet another flyer from the 'Maid's' breeding—Another Maid, winner of open handicaps from the age of eleven months.

Rosalie's Maid was put to Good as Gold and this produced no less than two Supreme Racing Champions, Gold Maid (bitch) and Gold Fame (dog), also a fine racer R. Ch. Rhinegold; in fact the whole litter was very useful.

From another branch of the 'Maid's' breeding came only one pup in Maid Marion's second litter to R. Ch. Strike Pay, and this turned out to be She's-a-Maid, who is dam of Merry Maid and R. Ch. Longfellow (sired by R. Ch. Yorky Boy).

Time and time again the consistency of the 'Maid' breeding has been proved.

MARRETTA

This prolific scratch winner—never beaten from scratch—had the bad luck to have Caesarean operations for her two litters. A Bilko cross greyhound offspring, Marretta was the first of a line of open whippets, her first (and best) litter consisting of Viva, Little Marretta, Majetta (all B.W.R.A. Racing Champions) and Hot Honey, also open class. Hot Honey was mated to R. Ch. Pedlar (El Diablo ex Cloey) and her pups included some very useful, though borderline dogs, also a 24-lb. bitch Pure Honey, who tragically died before reaching her full potential, but not before she had earned a big reputation on the open circuit. From Hot Honey's next litter to Wishy Was emerged the blue lightweight Honey Don't, British Open Champion, 1975.

R. Ch. Majetta has also produced open racing stock, and the only dog in Marretta's first litter, Viva, retired to stud duties after a successful open career.

VIV'S PET

Don Syson of Ilkeston W.R.C. has been a keen whippet owner for many years, in fact, he started whippet racing in 1964 with a

20-lb. brindle bitch, Viv's Pet, and when the time came to breed with her, the stud dog Robbo (litter brother to Little Mary and Cleo) was used, resulting in one dog and one bitch, a fawn brindle who weighed 24-lb. and was named Viv's Folly. Viv's Pet was again mated, this time to Blue Peter, and a 26-lb. blue bitch, Viv's Dream, was the outcome, an excellent sprinter.

A litter of seven pups produced by Viv's Folly was sired by R. Ch. Pedlar and this included Orlando, a good all-rounder, and Viv's Choice, who had a good share of open and club wins. A repeat of this mating included the 18-lb. Viv's Pride, who was a finalist on bends and straight in B.W.R.A. Championships.

When it came to breeding with Viv's Choice, the lightweight black dog R. Ch. Nip (Wishy Was ex R. Ch. Snowflake, winner of seven B.W.R.A. Champion titles, four straight, three bend) was selected and this brought the best litter bred by this kennel, as all eight pups were early winners and some went on to shine in open and B.W.R.A. racing.

By careful planning, Don Syson has succeeded in breeding good honest pups, and most of the dogs have two things in common: they are excellent trappers and always give of their best.

Chapter Ten

WHIPPET RACING 'GREATS'

LITTLE MARY

Bred in October 1964 out of Scarback, sired by the famous Bilko, Little Mary was, at 23 lb., the smallest in her litter. She was owned by Mr. Brian Cooper of Worsley near Manchester and this light fawn brindle was a most successful all-rounder. She was trained to run up tapes to the rag, but by the time she was twelve months, she had been introduced to the inside hare at Wigan Greyhound Stadium. Little Mary's first open win was at Darwin, Lancashire in August 1965, and this was the start of a fabulous open career during which she won approximately forty open weight races throughout the country.

Distance was irrelevant to this bitch who took almost every major trophy available during her racing career, whether over 100 yards or 350 yards! So high in her owner's esteem was Little Mary that an offer of £250 to buy her was refused.

BANG ON

This is a really famous name in the world of post-war whippet racing.

Bang On—a 31-lb. black bitch—was bred by Mr. T. Scott out of Gay Spot and sired by Bilko. Born in October 1963, this bitch was owned by Mr. G. F. Cumston. Her first open win was in August 1964 at Whaley Bridge, near Stockport, a really strong area for top-class racing whippets. Weighing 32 lb. for this particular event over the short distance of 150 yards, gives some indication of the power of this racer, then only ten months old.

Later in her career, she was to win three open events in eight days, starting with the Birmingham St. Leger, followed by the Kersall Weight Trophy and topping this with the Stewart Evans Trophy. In winning the Lancashire W.R.C. Tyldesley Rosebowl, she was handicapped to give 33 yards' start in the final over a distance of 150 yards—no mean feat. Years later, she still holds the Lancashire W.R.C. track record of 8·60 for 150 yards.

As many scratch races were, in those days, to a 30-lb. weight limit, George Cumston had no alternative but to turn to open scratch and, on her first attempt, Bang On won the All England Scratch Championship at Newcastle-upon-Tyne. During the next three years she won over seventy major scratch races, being beaten on three occasions only. She held track records at Stockport, New Mills and Lancashire W.R.C. and this at a time when other great dogs such as Irish Imp, White Rose, Darley Fly, Billie Can, Candy, El Diablo and Candyman were running, to name but a few. Many open and scratch wins are accredited to Bang On, a bitch whose legend still lives on.

Her blood is present in many of today's racing stock; her first litter to Blue Smoke produced Blue Max, himself an extremely good racer who could compete on equal terms with many top bitches. She was mated twice to R. Ch. Tinlegs, the first litter producing Spot On, a Tyne and Wear stud dog, following a successful scratch career; her litter in 1971 included the black dog R. Ch. He's-a-Dandy, an extremely useful open dog, later put at stud and now responsible for many open class whippets.

WISHY WAS

One of the most famous offspring from the great stud dog Blue Peter, was S. Ernest's Stoke dog Wishy Was, bred by Mr. Joe

Mather of Stockport out of a bitch named Blackie (not to be confused with Blackie from Ripon). Also in this litter, whelped in June 1965, was the bitch Bluebird, who lived in Yorkshire and raced with great success at open level, being the very first B.W.R.A. National Supreme Champion, at the First National Championships at Wetherby.

A black dog, Wishy Was weighed 26 lb. and had an enviable racing temperament which led to great consistency in racing. He was an excellent trapper and had stamina to spare. Trained and conditioned mainly to rag racing up tapes, he was a great sight to see, especially when he hit his rag at the finish. He sustained two serious leg injuries during his racing career, but it was an amputated toe which finally put paid to this.

Wishy Was must be ranked as one of the all-time greats, being one of the very few dogs who could compete with the top-class bitches which were around in those days. The dog was placed in about thirty opens, winning eighteen of them. After his great racing career, the inevitable step was to put the dog to stud duties, consequently Wishy Was blood flows through the veins of many of the dogs racing on our tracks today. Numerous open racers are included in his offspring. One unusual feature about the dog is that he really put his stamp on his pups colourwise, for only blue or black pups were ever bred from this prolific sire.

Good as Gold

Without any doubt, this stocky, fawn dog from Rochdale, Lancashire is the finest dog whippet ever to grace a racing track.

Mr. A. Walshaw of Manchester bred the litter in March 1969 out of Cleo (Bilko ex Scarback) sired by Golden Link, famous on the stud scene for siring winners with plenty of stamina. Also in the litter was Silver Dawn, who was bought by Mr. N. Pannell of Surrey and was also destined for fame and fortune, winning three racing champion titles in succession and being a notable open winner.

Peter Fitton purchased Good as Gold—pet name Randy—

when a four-month-old pup. Even as young as six months, Good as Gold was showing up well in puppy races, and it wasn't long before this powerful animal was taking on open dogs. His first open win came when he was twelve months old, at Hillstown, near Chesterfield and this triumph was followed by many more. In 1970, seventeen open wins were notched up; eighteen opens went his way in 1971; he had a total of nine in 1972 and the following year—even when the dog was over four years old and against fabulous competition—this phenomenal dog won four open handicaps.

Some of the dog's best performances were in May 1971 at Highgate Stadium when Good as Gold beat the legendary Little Lucy on a photo finish; he claimed the £50 purse at the All England 350 yards Sweepstake at Halifax Stadium in March 1971; he beat a field of the best in British whippet racing at Preston 150 yards open in June 1971, and in 1973 at the Lancaster open, he proved he could still take on the best and win.

Good as Gold's biggest claim to fame, however, was winning the British Whippet Racing Association Supreme Dog Champion title four years in succession, a feat which is unlikely to be achieved by any other whippet, dog or bitch. His first taste of B.W.R.A. success came at Ashington, Northumberland, in 1970 at his first attempt in Association racing; 1971 saw him repeat this honour at Measham, Leicestershire, and the following year spectators were astounded to see this plucky flyer pull off the hat-trick. He was, of course, one of the most popular dogs taking part in the 1973 Championships at Measham and, sure enough, victory was his again! Dogs have to qualify in their particular region for the National Championships, and only the cream of British whippets get through to the Finals; this gives an idea of the great talent of Good as Gold.

In view of his accomplishments on the track, there was plenty of demand for his services at stud, and Good as Gold became one of the most popular stud dogs in the country, following in the wake of those past stud 'greats' Blue Peter, Bilko, Wishy Was and Blue Fawn. There is little doubt that Good as Gold puts a very

1. Two very early whippeteers (about 1912) complete with 'cloth caps and mufflers'. These men were East Suffolk people, probably members of the Eastern Counties W.R.A. (*Photo: A. Rose, Eastleigh*)

2. Whippets rounding the bends at the B.W.R.A. Championships, Halifax Stadium, in 1974. (*Photo: D. Clark, Hertford*)

3. Dogs trapping in the scratch race for whippets clocking the fastest times at the B.W.R.A. Spring Classic, 1976. Winner was Demon in trap 1. (*Photo: D. Clark, Hertford*)

4. The start of a handicap race at Stevenage W.R.C. in 1971. (*Photo: D. Clark, Hertford*)

5. The Lancashire bitch Black County being weighed on spring-balance scales at the Aire Valley W.R.C. (*Photo: P. Wilson, Pudsey*)

6. Cheshire dog Hazel's Pal in full stride at the B.W.R.A. Spring Classic , April 1975. (*Photo: D. Clark, Hertford*)

7. Rag dogs taking part in the *North Western Evening Mail* Trophy event at Ulverston W.R.C. (*Photo:* Barrow News & Mail *Ltd.*)

8. One of the 'greats'—Little Mary poses with her collection of trophies.

9. R. Ch. Haymaker, formerly of the south, owned by D. Jennings under whose ownership he won the 22 lb. dog racing championship title in 1972 and 1973. Now owned by A. Redfearn of W. Yorkshire, he now enjoys a successful career at stud. (*Photo: D. Clark, Hertford*)

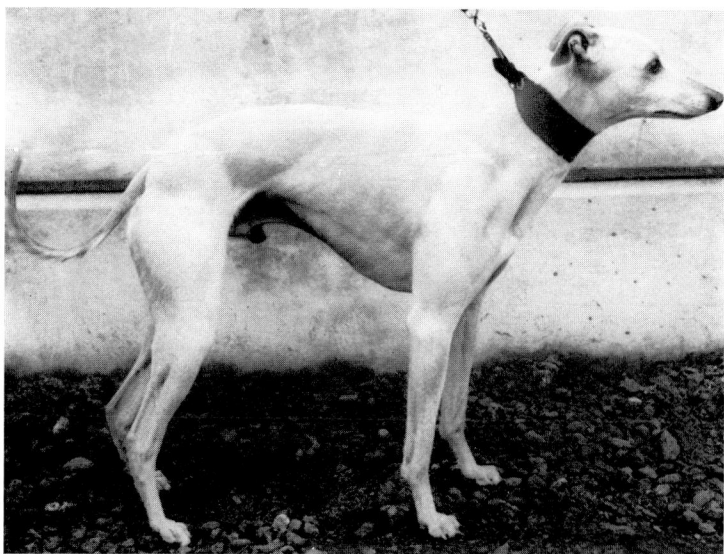

10. R. Ch. Good as Gold—winner of four supreme racing champion titles and prolific sire. (*Photo: P. Wilson, Pudsey*)

11. A trio of pedigree whippets from Mrs McKay's Laguna Kennels: Laguna Lilywhite, Ch. Laguna Light Lagoon and Laguna Lacquer. (*Photo: Lionel Young, Bristol*)

12. The top pedigree racer of 1976, T. Peart's R. Ch. Picketty Witch, winner of seven championship races.

13. Blue Streak at the B.F.S.S. Country Fair winning the up to 24 lb weight class in 1975. This pedigree whippet, owned by Mrs A. A. Gaitskell of London, has won once and been finalist twice at the W.C.R.A. Championships. He is also a show winner, has been to Crufts and is a coursing stake winner with the East of England W.C.C.

14. H. Field's southern pedigree bitch R. Ch. Peanut with a few of her many trophies.

15. The 1974 Greyhound Derby winner Jimsun (77 lb.) towers over the lightweight Evesham whippet R. Ch. Sidewinder (16 lb.) showing the vast difference in size. (*Photo: J. O'Bryne, Evesham, by courtesy of P. R. Sweeney, Rugby*)

16. Results indicator at the Furness W.R.C. (Rag Racing Club) (*Photo: I. Macdonald, Barrow-in-Furness*)

special stamp on pups from the right type of bitches, his offspring dominating the open race scene.

LITTLE LUCY

From a litter of four, bred by B. Leek of Bradford, Yorkshire in March 1968 out of Bilko and the fine brood bitch Young Lucy, two dogs were destined to become scratch racers, Warlord and the great Red Baron; a further dog pup died of distemper but Little Lucy, a black bitch, overcame the disease and went on to become one of the legendary 'greats'.

Lucy was owned by Mr. J. Simpson of Ripon, also owner of the famous stud dog Blue Fawn. She commenced her racing career at the tender age of seven months and was outstanding in Yorkshire League racing. It soon became obvious that she was a cut above average and this 25–26-lb. bitch won or was placed in innumerable open handicaps, varying from 130-yard sprints right up to 400-yard bend events. She pulled off a most amazing feat during a holiday weekend of racing, winning three opens in as many days: Barnsley 150 yards open (Priory W.R.C.), Hillstown 175 yards open, and Trawdon W.R.C. open at Colne, Lancs.

During her career, Lucy won approximately 100 opens on bends and straight; she has won scratch races and broken track records. Even after having two litters of pups and being past her peak, Little Lucy was capable of winning an open final.

In British Whippet Racing Association events, Little Lucy won the 28-lb. bitch Racing Champion title (300 yards bend), this was followed the same year by winning the 26-lb. straight title and taking the Supreme Champion crown at Ashington, Northumberland; in 1973 she won the 'Last Minute Trophy', which is a national bend event for veteran whippets of five years and over. Stamina she had a-plenty and a finer all-round racing whippet would be hard to find.

SNOWFLAKE

There are many in the whippet world who insist that Snowflake was the 'best ever'.

A white and fawn bitch bred by D. Sanderson of Kirkheaton, Yorkshire in August 1966, her sire was the inevitable Bilko and dam Snowball.

Mr. Arthur Ellis of Dewsbury purchased Snowflake and schooled her at the local whippet club on Sands Lane Playing Fields, together with litter brother White Wings. Club handicap wins came her way when she was eight months old and it didn't take her long to claim scratch champion titles at Dewsbury and Kirkheaton clubs—and this weighing a mere 22–23 lb!

This incredible bitch's first open win was at Hillstown, a club where she was eventually destined to win five opens and gain one runner-up placing from six opens entered. Also at Hillstown, she twice won the 32-lb. limit scratch race, which gives an idea of the power behind this fine animal. Her racing champion title came at the very first B.W.R.A. National Finals when she took the 24-lb title.

Snowflake's career can only be described as brilliant, winning over fifty opens at a time when opens were much scarcer than in present-day whippet racing. She held track records and won open scratch races; competition was excellent too, with such racers as rag dogs Little Tipsy and Wishy Was, also those two outstanding Ripon whippets Blackie and Little Lucy.

In team racing, Snowflake was a dependable member of the strong Dewsbury contingent in Yorkshire League racing, when Dewsbury won the championship three times in succession—no surprise with such team members as Snowflake, Petra, Fawn Lady, Blue Cloud, Dolly Blue, Blackjack, Little Bess, Smoke-Ring and R. Ch. Blue Max. Dewsbury's scratch championship belonged to Snowflake between 1968 and 1970, also a track record time of 10·16 for 175 yards.

After a litter of pups (which included the 16-lb. black dog Nip

62

who was to have a successful career at stud after a glowing racing record), Snowflake again returned to the track to win Swallownest (Sheffield) open, and a weight class event at Southend.

A lightweight whippet who took on heavyweights on equal terms and showed them the way home, Snowflake died in November 1974, leaving a racing record still to be equalled.

PEDLAR

One of an incredible litter of four dogs whelped in July 1967, the others being R. Ch. Tinlegs, Bramble Star and Crazy Horse. This was the only litter bred out of Cleo, sired by El Diablo (Bilko ex Alma), more's the pity. A handsome leggy brindle, Pedlar was a great character, much respected on the open circuit at a time when many excellent runners were around: Blackie, Wishy Was, Little Lucy, Magpie and Roberta D. Pedlar didn't miss a chance to snatch an open final and, had there been segregated opens around at the time, doubtless his fame would have spread even more.

Three B.W.R.A. 28-lb. dog titles were claimed by Pedlar, and he was Supreme Dog Champion at Watford in 1969.

Possessing such good bloodlines, it was obvious his stud services were going to be popular and the dog has sired numerous top-grade whippets.

Although his original owner, Chris Wileman, later emigrated, the dog remains in England to further enhance racing whippet stock.

ROBERTA D

A very popular lightweight brindle bitch owned by J. and C. Dolan of Stockport, Cheshire, Roberta D was the B.W.R.A. Supreme Champion at the Second National Championships in 1969 at Watford, Herts.

She was whelped in March 1968 out of Brindle Bandit, sired by Robbo (Bilko ex Scarback), but had the misfortune to break a leg at eight weeks old. An early first season, followed by an accident which resulted in a ripped chest necessitating eighteen stitches, meant that Roberta D faced more than her share of setbacks before finally being launched into racing. However, this story had a happy ending as she won her first open handicap at Church Gresley W.R.C., Leicestershire, aged fourteen months and never looked back.

Her reserves of stamina ensured that she reached many open finals. She also loved bend racing, although this was not as popular then as it now is. A year after her Straight Championships success, Roberta D added the 20-lb. Bend Racing Champion title to her string of honours, and in 1971 she took the 22-lb. bend title.

After a dazzling racing career, Roberta D was used for breeding and her first litter, sired by the Yorkshire stud dog Smoke-Ring (Fawn Eagle ex Smokey Girl), included open winners, the most notable being Pendle Witch and R. Ch. Trebora. A later litter sired by Good as Gold included a really top-class dog, Mickey D, winner of open honours, bend and straight.

The Dolan brothers have raced whippets for many years and the list of winners—Roberta D, R. Ch. Ruby D, Mickey D—testify as to the amount of work they are prepared to put in in order to enjoy their pastime to the full.

BLACKIE

Every whippet enthusiast has a favourite amongst the 'great' racers past and present, and this heavyweight bitch owned by Mr. and Mrs. K. Arnold of Ripon is mine.

She was whelped in November 1967 out of Golden Wyn, sired by Blue Fawn, and was actually named just before she was born, as a black nose and muzzle was seen to appear; eventually she emerged into the world, a light fawn with black muzzle, but the name 'Blackie' stuck and was destined to become really well known. This excellent bitch was a real spectacle to watch when she was on form (as she invariably was), leaving the scratch box and gradually overhauling the rest of the runners to win time and time again. Blackie—100 per cent honest—had to be seen to be believed, so it's not surprising that she smashed many track records and gained countless victories in opens from short sprints to 200 yards, also finding success in scratch racing. In B.W.R.A. racing Blackie won the straight 32-lb. bitch title at the 1971 Championships, towards the end of a colourful racing career.

Blackie had litters to various sires, her best progeny being the Sheffield bitch R. Ch. Pedlackie (sired by R. Ch. Pedlar) and the Lancashire dog Jackson (sired by Kaz-Garas) who was killed by a loose dog while racing.

CHERRY

Looking rather like a miniature version of Blackie—light fawn with black muzzle—Cherry was from the second litter out of Golden Wyn, but sired by Darley Fly (Bilko ex Tearaway) and whelped in October 1968.

Cherry was owned by Mr. A. Pickup of Ripon and was to be seen regularly at open meetings, when this 20-pounder could be relied upon to give a cracking display of racing from the front. Although a bit temperamental at times and hesitating at the finish, Cherry won a remarkable number of opens and it would be hard to imagine the number she would have won, had she run through every time. Cherry's first straight Racing Champion title was earned at Ashington, Northumberland, in 1970, but 1971 was her best year when she again won the 20-lb. title, then took the Supreme Champion award. Also in 1971, Cherry was the top whippet in British open racing.

An exceptional little racer, still much talked about.

WENDYGO

There are plenty of racing dogs on today's whippet tracks who have been crossed with greyhound blood, but one of the first (and one of the very best) was the 21-lb. black bitch Wendygo owned by Mr. I. Crawshaw of Halifax, West Yorkshire.

She was bred in May 1970 out of a small greyhound bitch named Shirley Girl and sired by R. Ch. Yorky Boy, a lightweight whippet dog, and the resulting litter ensured a lucrative stud career for Yorky Boy as a suitable mate for the small greyhound bitches.

At an early age Wendygo showed promise and her first open win came when she was just twelve months old, winning the Aire Valley open handicap at Bingley, Yorkshire. An extremely good relationship between owner and dog meant that the bitch could be relied upon to give of her best, and countless opens were taken by Wendygo during her racing years, in spite of having a long layoff due to injury at one period. In the National Top Ten competition this black bitch reached third place in 1971 and 1973, and seventh in 1972. At the 1973 B.W.R.A. National Championships, Wendygo took the 22-lb. Bitch Champion title, then went on to become a very popular Supreme Champion, beating that superlative dog Good as Gold in the final run-off.

She was still performing with style at open level at six years old and after a litter of pups to Good as Gold.

DASHER

One of the more modern whippet racing 'legends' is this 19-lb. blue bitch bred in March 1971 by C. Huskins of Normanton, Yorkshire out of Morning Star, sired by the Yorkshire stud dog Seiko (Bilko ex Roanbar Babette).

Even as young as six and a half months old, this flyer was winning heats in open handicaps, consequently it wasn't long before she claimed her first open of many.

Her owners, Mr. and Mrs. R. Hodgson of Normanton, were dedicated to the task of training and racing Dasher, also her kennelmate Lasher, and soon the bitch was adding B.W.R.A. honours to her list of achievements. In 1972 she won the 20-lb. title and became Supreme Champion, also in 1972 she won the Top Ten competition, having more points in open racing that year than any other whippet. The year 1973 saw her again pull off the double, winning the 20-lb. title at Measham and also the Top Ten. It was a B.W.R.A. hat-trick when Dasher again took the 20-lb. title in 1974, but this year she had to be content with second place in the Top Ten competition.

Dasher was one of the most consistent straight racers; she never seemed fatigued and would race on two or even three consecutive days and still be triumphant in each instance. For sheer stamina and gameness, lots of people say Dasher was the best, and I think they are very probably right!

After a dazzling career, Dasher had three pups to R. Ch. Haymaker (Wishy Was ex Surprise).

SING ON

One of the most famous whippets in the South of England must be the 22-lb. blue dog Sing On, bred from equally well-known parents, the Stoke dog Wishy Was, out of Stevenage parti-coloured bitch She Sings, who herself possessed great open talent.

Two from the September 1972 litter made open class, the black Stoke dog R. Ch. Holly Lane and Sing On, but it was the latter dog who was destined for the real big time. During his peak, Sing On really shone at open level, not only in the south, for the dog also travelled far north to participate. So good was his open record that the dog twice reached the British Top Ten, a remark-able achievement for a dog whippet. Another double this light-weight dog has pulled off is to become B.W.R.A. Supreme Champion Dog twice, in 1974 (beaten only by Supreme bitch Gold Maid) and in 1976 when the Supreme Bitch Coconut won the final run-off. Sing On has, in fact, three B.W.R.A. Racing Champion titles as he also took the 22-lb. straight champion title in 1975, making three titles on the trot.

Early in his stud career, Sing On's progeny has been seen to possess class.

KELLY GOLD

Mr. A. Daughtrey of Wakefield, Yorkshire owns and bred this 18-lb. fawn bitch, whelped in April 1973 out of his whippet Kelly's Eye—a prolific open finalist—sired by R. Ch. Good as Gold.

The only bitch out of a litter of four, Kelly Gold suffered an early setback when she broke a leg at six months old, but overcame this hurdle and was amongst the Top Ten whippets in 1974 1975 and 1976, also winning the B.W.R.A. 18-lb. bitch Racing Champion title in 1975 and 1976 when she went on to become runner-up to Supreme bitch Coconut.

Compared to the average open class racing whippet, Kelly Gold has been lightly raced, yet has still managed to be one of the country's leading racers.

WHAT-A-MAID

Bred from a strong line of excellent racing stock, this lightweight fawn bitch—along with litter sister Tracy's Maid, a lightweight black—took the open circuit by storm, causing whippet enthusiasts to look twice!

The bitch is owned by D. Ashley of Nottinghamshire and was bred in April 1973 out of Julie's Maid, sired by the Preston stud dog Kaz-Garas. Her first open win came at fourteen months, since when she has won a stack of opens and various placings. What-a-Maid is equally at home on bends and straight; she holds 20-lb. Bitch Champion titles for B.W.R.A. bends and straight National Finals, won in 1975 and 1976 respectively.

In open racing, What-a-Maid really showed the way home: in 1974 she was ninth out of all Britain in the national points competition which takes in dogs' performances throughout a year's racing; in 1975 she was runner-up in the same competition, and in 1976 she managed the runners-up placing again, even after a considerable layoff due to injury.

As an all-rounder, she was one of the best!

Chapter Eleven

PEDIGREE WHIPPET RACING

The Whippet Club is the senior breed club and was founded in 1899; its patron is Her Grace the Duchess of Devonshire and its President the Hon. A. Mackay.

The object of this club, as stated in its rules, is: 'To promote the breeding of whippets by endeavouring to make the qualities and type of the breed as defined by The Kennel Club Standards better known; to define precisely and publish a description of same and to urge the adoption of such type upon breeders, judges and dog show committees as the only recognised and unvarying standards by which whippets are to be judged and which should in future be uniformly accepted as the sole standards of excellence in breeding and in awarding prizes of merit to whippets.'

In view of the growing interest in racing for pedigree whippets and in order to prevent a divergence of type in the breed between show and racing whippets, the Whippet Club formed a sub-committee to develop an organisation to act as a governing body for pedigree whippet racing.

The Whippet Club Racing Association was founded from this sub-committee headed by Mr. Norman Odell, and the first meeting of the sub-committee was held on 21 April 1968 when Mr. Odell opened by saying that, as the oldest breed club, he felt that the Whippet Club should take the initiative and standardise a set of rules for British whippet racing. Mrs. Joanna

69

Russell was appointed Secretary of the sub-committee and by 23 February 1969, at the sixth meeting, a framework of rules was adopted and it was decided to form the Whippet Club Racing Association. Mr. George McCourt was appointed racing manager for the Association.

It was decided that membership of the Association should be by the club rather than by individuals or dogs, and each club secretary should apply to Mrs. Russell for registration forms for every dog belonging to the club, these to be filled in and sent back with Kennel Club registration certificates. If approved, W.C.R.A. passports, numbered on a yearly basis, would then be returned to the club secretaries.

At the tenth meeting on 15 March 1970, Mr. Norman Odell had to resign as Chairman since he was going to live in America, and he was succeeded by Mr. George McCourt.

The first W.C.R.A. open race meeting was held at Bracknell Sports Centre, Berkshire on 16 May 1970 when W.C.R.A. passports were required for all whippets and the weight groups were under 18 lb., 18 to 21 lb., 21 to 24 lb., 24 to 27 lb. and 27 to 30 lb. Trophies were awarded, together with embroidered coats in velvet for the winners of each weight group.

At the fifteenth meeting on 16 April 1971, it was suggested that if a whippet should win two finals at two W.C.R.A. open events, it should be given the title 'Track Champion'. Subsequently the Whippet Club received permission from the Kennel Club to grant the title 'Whippet Club Racing Champion'. A whippet can gain the title by winning two finals regardless of the weight group, also the finals can, and have been, won on bends or straights or one of each.

At the earlier Championship meetings, officials were either members of the W.C.R.A. committee or were recruited by them from the racing clubs they attended. Mr. George McCourt, as racing manager, had been responsible for welding the W.C.R.A. into a functioning unit.

A letter of resignation as Chairman and racing manager from Mr. McCourt led to Mrs. D. U. McKay being unanimously elected as Chairman on 1 August 1971, and on 23 January 1972 Mr. Peter Spokes took over the duties of secretary and racing manager.

Due to the enormous improvement in the quality of the Championship meetings held over the last eighteen months, it was agreed that four meetings should be held annually, two over 240 yards bends and two 150 yards straights.

For 1974 Mr. Charlie Redknap took over as racing manager for four Championship meetings, all of which were held on a neutral ground at Abbotts Ann, near Andover. In 1975, four similar Championship meetings were again held at Abbotts Ann.

Mr. Peter Spokes took over the duties of racing manager for 1976, his wife Pamela being the secretary for the W.C.R.A. committee.

Whippet racing clubs affiliated to the W.C.R.A. have their own constitution and rules according to their own requirements, but many of them require the whippets to be eligible for a W.C.R.A. passport. The passport is also the usual qualification required when a club puts on an open meeting.

Most clubs cater for every grade of whippet with regular racing to a club handicap based on a whippet's performance, so that everyone has a chance to win during the season. Trophy meetings within the club are usually on a yard per pound basis, with the trophies being held annually and a smaller trophy being given to keep. Clubs do not generally give cash prizes and gambling, as a rule, is prohibited.

A rosette or medal is normally given to the winner of each race at ordinary meetings and usually there is either a points system for one or more trophies at the end of the season, or trophies are given for five or ten wins, or similar numbers. It is not usual to run an ordinary meeting to find one overall winner, although there may be two or three group finals based either on club handicaps or weights.

Four-dog races are the most common practice, though some clubs with large memberships run five- or six-dog races. The clubs take a pride in having a well-marked track with tapes or fencing, depending on whether the track is permanent or not. It is usual to have a paddock for gathering the whippets prior to a race, clear results boards, printed programmes (entries being made prior to the meeting); most have electrically operated traps, some have electronic timing, photo-finish equipment, public address systems, and refreshment and toilet facilities are provided wherever possible.

The type of track, i.e. bends or straight, and distances, depend on the ground which the club has available. Straights of 150, 175 and 200 yards are run, two-bend distances vary from 240 to 300 yards and there are four-bend 350-yard races. If a club has the facilities it will vary the distances and types of racing, and before a Championship meeting will do its best to give its members racing over the distance that is forthcoming. Some clubs have experimented with hurdle racing.

Club trophies are usually donated by a member who will probably express a preference for the type of racing; this may be for the best whippet at yard per pound over a shorter distance, or $1\frac{1}{2}$ yards per pound over a longer distance, best on club handicap, best dog or best bitch, pairs racing, a points basis or puppy or veteran trophies. The club provides the smaller trophy for the owner to keep.

Facilities for trialling puppies are usually given during the interval and some clubs will have midweek evening meetings during the season, or an hour before the racing to carry out the necessary training. Members are not encouraged to race their dogs before they are twelve months old.

Most enthusiasts belong to more than one club, and neighbouring clubs usually try to arrange their programmes so that they do not clash. The clubs draw up their programmes for the year and these are usually printed and given to members at the start of the season. Meetings are generally once a fortnight and some clubs meet throughout the year, weather permitting, while others have a shorter season.

Matches between clubs are popular, the clubs usually joining together to provide a trophy which is competed for on a home and away basis, and the race winners receiving trophies supplied by the home club from entry fees.

Practically all the pedigree racing whippets are house pets, the kennel dogs are in the house during the day and owners love their whippets for themselves. Training and feeding are taken seriously, three to five miles being the usual daily road walk, apart from free exercise. Everyone has his own ideas on the correct diet for a racing dog.

Generally a litter is only bred when the owner wants a puppy.

Race meetings are a family affair and in general a very friendly sporting atmosphere prevails. At ordinary club handicap meetings the club whippet has its day, racing champions finding it as hard as the rest to get a win, and interest is keen as to who can win on the current handicap. The racing is watched throughout to see the new youngster coming on, the veteran still coming through, and whether a dog can still make it from scratch when giving an extra yard.

Trophy meetings, of course, have the excitement of seeing the best whippets coming through and, even though each owner has got the dog in its best form to win, the merit of a good whippet is appreciated and ungrudging congratulations are freely given to the winner.

Open meetings are becoming more popular and numerous each year, and the *Whippet News* Pedigree Top Ten competition started in 1976 has aroused great interest in these events. Here again, most of the competitors are well known to each other and a friendly spirit prevails.

Occasionally, a club will put on racing for a charity or local occasion such as a fête where there is a totalisator, and Surrey W.R.C. have Bank Holiday open meetings over varied distances with a tote, but these are exceptions, and it is widely felt that to introduce cash prizes or gambling would destroy the sporting spirit of the racing, where the interest is centred entirely on the whippets and interest is concentrated on producing the best just to fulfil the ambition of having the best.

The ordinary whippet can give just as much pride and pleasure to the owner, because these dogs keep the clubs going while the stars are away at opens, and they are given every encouragement to win. Veterans of six years old and more are still kept fit to enjoy their racing and many clubs make a feature of special races for veterans at yard per pound (as the distance is limited for them) and yard per year over six years old.

At W.C.R.A. Championship meetings, the clubs give good support to dogs owned by their members, and each club hopes to be well represented in the finals.

CLUBS ON THE PEDIGREE CIRCUIT

ANDOVER & DISTRICT W.R.C.

The club was formed in the spring of 1972, the first meeting being held on 9 April 1972 at Middle Wallop, where racing still continues to be held fortnightly throughout the year with the exception of January and February, when meetings are held monthly. Approximately twenty meetings per year are held at Middle Wallop and approximately ten other charity meetings at a variety of local venues, in between normal racing dates.

No cash prizes are given, but the club has forty-two annual returnable trophies, and all finalists are presented with rosettes. The trophies are competed for over a variety of distances, straight 100, 150, 160, 175 and 200 yards. Bend racing (conventional U-shaped bend, outside lure) is held over 200, 240, 250, 275 and 300 yards. All dogs must be registered with the W.C.R.A. and dogs under one year are allowed to trial and begin racing provided they have a Class 1 K.C. registration. Andover has a large contingent of Whippet Club Racing Champions who race regularly with the club, its most famous celebrity being W. C. Racing Champion Picketty Witch, winner of seven Championships.

It has not been necessary to increase prices since the formation of the club.

Oxford W.R.C.

Formed in September 1970 by Ernest Glaholm, Tom Savage, Peter and Pam Spokes and Neil James at the Gosford All Blacks Rugby Football Club, Kidlington, there were five whippets at the first meeting held over 175 yards straight.

Membership steadily increased, with racing on Sunday mornings, and at the end of 1971 the club moved to its present site on Botley Road, Oxford, where it boasts a bends track of 240 to 300 yards and a straight track up to 160 yards.

Since May 1972 a number of W.C.R.A. Championships have been held on the 240-yard bends track and open meetings are held every year. The club aims to provide well-organised racing for Class 1 pedigree whippets in a friendly family atmosphere; there are no money prizes and betting is forbidden. Prizes are trophies, shields or rosettes and the club is well endowed with annual trophies. Racing is usually held on alternate Sunday afternoons, and whippet racing displays are also staged at country shows and fêtes.

Oxford Club is affiliated to the Whippet Club Racing Association, so all whippets must have a Class 1 registration and hold a W.C.R.A. passport. Club whippets must not exceed 32 lb. weight nor 21 inches shoulder height.

On club racing days, dogs run off their club handicap, expressed in yards relative to scratch. There is always a dog of the day competition in two weight divisions. Club handicaps are revised after each club meeting, i.e. dogs winning in the first round are handicapped 2 yards, semi-final winners are handicapped another yard and the winner of the final a further yard. This system is designed to give as many whippets as possible a chance to win, and prevent any one dog dominating the prizes for long. The yard per pound handicap system is used for most club trophies.

Prospective members are allowed to attend two race meetings and then may apply to join the club, a majority vote at the committee meeting being required to admit new members.

Mrs. D. U. McKay, Chairman of the W.C.R.A., is club President and has been an active and winning member for years. Secretary/Treasurer is Mrs. P. Spokes.

NEW FOREST W.R.C.

The first in this area, the club started in the early 1960s in the heart of the Forest at Stoney Cross, a disused aerodrome which the club was allowed to use by the New Forest Council at a low yearly rental. In 1965 the first South Coast Championships were held at Beaulieu and continued later at Fawley.

The club was founded and run by Mr. George McCourt who was instrumental in founding the racing side of the Whippet Club and in 1968 organised the racing track layout and running of the first W.C.R.A. open meeting at Bracknell in May 1970.

Due to a change of venue, the title of the club later altered to Southampton & District W.R.C.

SURREY W.R.C.

The Surrey club was formed in the summer of 1969 by Colin and Pauline Noon of the Novakula Kennel, and Frank Tanner, with the assistance of Jack and Vi Noon. Through an introduction by June Minns and with Frank providing the traps and Colin and Pauline providing the rest of the equipment and management, the club started trials meetings in a field at Chessington over a straight 200-yard uphill track.

Following negotiations with the Leatherhead U.D.C. the club, which by now had started racing in earnest with some thirty whippets competing in club meetings, moved in the spring of 1970 to Fetcham Grove (now the leisure centre) and racing continued here, mainly on a straight 150-yard track until the club again moved its venue to the present location of the Riverside Club, Fetcham, near Leatherhead at the beginning of 1973.

Track layouts have changed during the time of the club's existence, culminating in the present set-up of the ever-popular

150-yard straight, a 240-yard two-bend and a 350-yard four-bend layout (both bend-tracks using the inside lure system) and a 100-yard hurdles track.

With six electrically operated traps, electronic timing, a public address system and an 8-ft. elevated lure driver's stand, the club is well equipped to cater for anything from club to Championship meetings and open events.

Racing at club meetings is roughly divided throughout the season between weight and graded racing, 150 and 240 yards being run at one yard per pound and 350-yard racing at $1\frac{1}{2}$ yards per pound for weight competition. The graded system is left exclusively to the handicapper who uses the whippet's best form in assessing its handicap which is re-assessed from meeting to meeting.

WHIPPET CLUB OF SCOTLAND RACING SECTION

This is primarily a social club, and although possibly one of the smallest pedigree racing clubs, is, however, the only K.C. Registered Breed Club to have a racing section. It was inspired by a picnic outing held at Innerleithen during which bewildered owners tried to persuade equally bewildered dogs to 'rag'.

In the late 1960s the treasurer and secretary of the club, Mr. and Mrs. D. F. Lindsay, supported by Mrs. E. Third, formed a racing section which met once a month from April to September at Blair Drummond, near Stirling; the dogs were hand-slipped to a hand-operated lure. Blair Drummond then became a Safari Park and the whippets withdrew to the neighbouring estate of Ochtertyre, which is probably the most scenically beautiful and the bumpiest of all venues.

Manually operated traps were bought and racing was over 150 yards with handicapping at one yard per pound. However, it soon became clear that the same whippets were winning too consistently to maintain the interest of the less successful, and the club was fortunate to be joined by handicapper Mrs. 'Patsy' Thompson, who in 1972 introduced a successful penalty system.

Annual trophies for the best dog and bitch are competed for on points gained in this handicapping system, and meetings are held every third Sunday from May to November with a turnout of twenty to thirty dogs. Rosettes are competed for at each meeting.

The club is affiliated to the W.C.R.A., the only K.C. Registered Breed Club to do so. Several of its members are also members of British Whippet Racing Association registered clubs. The club also has happy relations with the B.W.R.A. registered Tayside W.R.C. and has had several interclub matches. Although under a considerable geographical handicap, a few of the club's dogs have journeyed to the southern counties with some success and some have qualified for the B.W.R.A. Championships on straights and bends.

Some of this Scottish club's notable winners are M. Flosshilde (Flossy), M. Dorabella (Dottybelle), Farmacy Christmas Fayre (Flip), M. Sandman (Hazy), Shane, M. Lode (Rochet), Sabre, Sweeney, Bugs Bunny, Midge, Bruntsfield Wee Bogle (Tessa), Ringmore Old Silver (Puma), Rocket, M. Dutchman (Smoksey) and M. Sparafucile (Spara), all having gained honours in W.C.R.A., open or trophy racing.

TAMWORTH W.R.C.

Founded in October 1971, this club runs predominantly bend meetings, but changes to straight racing before the W.C.R.A. Straight Championships so that the dogs are familiar with the type of racing.

The handicap system is usually 1 yard per pound, but there are approximately twenty-five trophies which are run for annually, some scratch, some $\frac{1}{2}$ yard per pound, 1 yard per pound or $1\frac{1}{2}$ yards per pound and one is run on a time handicap.

Racing takes place every week from February to November for trophies, rosettes or shields; in addition there is a points system to find the best dog and bitch of every eight weeks and the top dog and bitch for the year, and there is also a chart for veteran points.

Maidstone & Mid-Kent W.R.C.

The club germinated from the enthusiasm of three members of the then East Sussex W.R.C. who raced on the old Lewes Racecourse.

Three members, Mr. Charles Stone, Arnold Mortimer and Alan Jones, enjoyed their racing but considered the possibility of starting a club in Kent, not only to cut down on travelling time but also, they hoped, to instil some country interest in the sport. All this took place in June 1972 and the Maidstone & Mid-Kent W.R.C. came into being and held its first meeting in the grounds of the Boxley Manor Country Club, just outside Maidstone, in October of the same year. A change of ground in 1974 saw racing move to Yelsted on the old Detling Aerodrome.

The meetings cover the whole spectrum of events during the season with 12-yard dashes, 100- and 120-yard sprints, 150-yard straights, 240- and 350-yard bends over their permanent Hughenholtz track. Outside commitments are also undertaken, with exhibition and charity racing. Weight class, yard, $\frac{1}{2}$ yard and $1\frac{1}{2}$ yards per pound and time racing all find space in the club's fixture list for its fortnightly meetings from March to November.

East Sussex W.R.C.

A couple of show-going lady whippeteers found the excitement of whippet racing a refreshing change from the ardours of showing, consequently the East Sussex Club was formed in 1969.

A very interested following quickly accumulated in this relatively new southern sport and many weekends were spent on Lewes Racecourse training dogs in the art of trapping and chasing with the aid of some hand-operated traps and a lure driven by a bicycle wheel. Interest rapidly grew, a committee was formed and a varied racecard was produced. The club soon became fully mechanised with an electrically driven lure machine and traps, racing being over a straight course of either 100, 150 or 200 yards and later over 240-yard bends.

This club has grown by leaps and bounds, the general public of Sussex becoming more and more aware of whippet racing, new members turning up week after week. Racing is held on Sunday afternoons every two weeks from March to November on the Plumpton Racecourse, where many young whippets are fast finding fame in the sporting world.

W.C.R.A. PASSPORTS

All pedigree racing whippets registered with the W.C.R.A. are derived from show stock registered with the Kennel Club. Before 1 April 1976, subject to fulfilling the requirements of the Kennel Club regarding the registration of its parents, a puppy would be issued with a Class 1 registration card showing its breed, sex, colour, date of birth, sire, dam, breeder, owner, name and Kennel Club registration number.

The minimum requirements for registration of whippets with the Whippet Club Racing Association are: (1) Class 1 Kennel Club Registration, and (2) five registrations of registered breeding acceptable to the Whippet Club Racing Association Committee. The committee shall, however, have the right without reservation to refuse the registration of any dog or bitch without being liable to give the owner any reason whatsoever, and the decision of the committee is final and binding at all times.

From 1 April 1976 the Kennel Club register was divided into two sections, the Basic Register in which all dogs are included, registered with name, details of parentage, sex, colour, breeder, date of birth and individual number; the Active Register, into which a dog which its owner decides to show or enter for competition, breed from or export, must be advanced. All dogs registered before 1 April 1976 were automatically included in the Active Register.

The requirements of the W.C.R.A. for a passport application will in future require Kennel Club Basic Registration under (1).

Many breeders register their own affix with the Kennel Club as, when this is granted, no other person may use it, and it serves to identify their dogs. Passports are issued in the Kennel Club registered name and owners use either a shortened form of this or a racing name at their clubs, but the full K.C. name is used for Championship meetings.

An application for a W.C.R.A. passport requires the signature of the breeder of the whippet, plus a seconder from a list issued by the W.C.R.A. of approved persons. No passport is issued until the whippet is twelve calendar months old, as a whippet under this age cannot run in any race conducted under the Rules of Racing of the W.C.R.A. The passport itself is in book form, the centre pages containing four outline views of the whippet which must be filled in with details of colour and marks, and details of toes and toenails, this being signed as true by the club secretary or a person on the approved list.

At one time, all races run by the whippet under W.C.R.A. Rules of Racing were entered on the passport, but now only Championship Finals results are shown.

The maximum height of a whippet eligible for W.C.R.A. registration is 21 inches at the shoulder; it must have been duly vaccinated against the recognised canine diseases of distemper, contagious hepatitis and leptospira canicola (*L. icterohaemorrhagiae*).

When applying for a passport, owners must also supply the Kennel Club card showing transfer of ownership where applicable, and must notify the secretary of the W.C.R.A. of the sale or death of any registered whippet.

Some affixes well known in pedigree whippet racing:

Affix	*Breeder*
Tweseldown	Lady Anderson
Springharn	Miss P. Batty
Casaloma	Mrs. C. England
Wirrawon	Miss J. Fisher
Franciscan	Mrs. C. Francis
Welstar	Mrs. L. Jones

81

Affix	*Breeder*
Karyon	Mrs. J. Keable
Nimrodel	Mrs. I. H. Lowe
Laguna	Mrs. D. U. McKay
Chancerick	Mrs. H. Meek and Mrs. B. Griffith
Novakula	Mr. and Mrs. C. Noon
Ricardo	Mrs. E. Richardson
Russetwood	Miss B. V. Rooney
Martinsell	Mrs. J. Russell and Mrs. C. Brown
Selbrook	Mr. D. Selby and Mrs. J. Selby
Papedaro	Mr. and Mrs. P. Spokes
Taimo	Commander and Mrs. Stubbs
Fulmen	Mr. and Mrs. Watts
Shalfleet	Mrs. Wilton-Clark
Trackmaster	Mr. J. Wiltshire
Crawshaw	Miss M. Wright

CHAMPIONSHIP RACE MEETINGS

Up to 1977, no qualification has been required for a whippet to run at a Championship meeting apart from the possession of a W.C.R.A. passport and membership of the owner to a club affiliated to the W.C.R.A.

Dogs and bitches are not separated in the racing. In the earlier days of the W.C.R.A. there was a danger of insufficient entrants in each weight group to make the Championship meaningful, but nowadays there is a distinct possibility that entries may have to be pruned. When the entries began to increase noticeably, a meeting of the committee decided that five-dog races should be held, with firsts and seconds going through to the next round. The weight groups are now 16, 18, 20, 22, 24, 26, 28 and up to 30 lbs. All dogs are weighed-in up to one hour before the racing and one ounce overweight will disqualify a whippet from running, although there is no disqualification if it is below weight, i.e. a dog weighing 21 lb. can run in the up to 24-lb. group.

All racing is from scratch and racing at both Championship meetings and pedigree clubs is always to the lure, and ragging is not allowed.

Affiliated clubs are each required to supply at least one experienced official and W.C.R.A. committee members also act as officials.

Entries are made in advance of the meeting and a public draw is held; this is made by numbers, starting from the final of each weight group and working back to the first heats, so that the dogs are not identified until the draw is finished.

In general, with firsts and seconds going through, a whippet has to run a heat, a semi-final and a final but, in some of the more congested weight groups, quarter-finals are also necessary. The number of entries in each Championship for 1976 was around 200, which meant 80 to 90 races to get through during the day.

A public address system is in operation to call the dogs to the paddock and announce results. In the paddock, stewards check each dog against its passport. Three finish judges, all on the same side of the line and including a timekeeper, agree on the result of each race, and this is then written in triplicate and dispatched to the public address and results boards, together with the time.

Trophies for first, second, third and fourth places in each weight group are presented to the finalists and each first heat winner receives a rosette. When a whippet has won two finals and becomes a W.C.R.A. Champion, the owner is presented with a framed Certificate of Championship. Since the W.C.R.A. Championships began, there have been forty-three Champions made up, but this achievement is becoming increasingly more difficult as only five new W.C.R.A. Championships were achieved during 1976.

The pattern of Championship racing has developed into two straight meetings and two bends each year. The straights are generally over 150 yards, although it is anticipated that 175 yards will be tried as an experiment; the other two meetings are round two bends over 240 yards.

The ultimate aim of the W.C.R.A. is to have its own neutral

permanent ground for Championships, with storage facilities for its own equipment. Until this becomes a viable proposition, however, a neutral ground is used when it is available and within practical reach of the officials responsible for setting up the track and conveying equipment. Otherwise, affiliated clubs put on a Championship meeting and are responsible for track layout and equipment, whilst the W.C.R.A. officials are responsible for the actual racing.

OPEN POINTS COMPETITION

A contest aimed to determine the most successful whippets in W.C.R.A. open events each season was inaugurated in 1976. Known as the *Whippet News* Pedigree Racing Top Ten, this is based on the similar competition run by *Whippet News* for whippets racing under B.W.R.A. rules.

All open events which are run off to a final, plus the four W.C.R.A. Championships, are counted. Whippets are awarded points for heat wins, weight group final placings or, in the case of events run to a final between all the weight group winners, points are awarded to overall finalists.

The whippet scoring most points holds for one year a trophy jointly presented by *Whippet News* and Mr. Vic Granger, and the remaining nine whippets receive a certificate.

The number of eligible events held the first year was fifteen, a record number for pedigree racing. Because the pedigree clubs are scattered, with big distances to be travelled by most entrants, scoring is limited to a whippet's best ten results. This also helps owners of whippets injured or of bitches who come into season during the summer months, in that they are usually still able to collect scores from the maximum ten events.

Chapter Twelve

BREEDERS OF OUTSTANDING PEDIGREE STOCK

CHANCERICK WHIPPETS

Mr. and Mrs. R. Meek bought their first whippet, Chisige Ricky, in 1966 and were introduced to whippet racing by Mrs. Barbara Griffith who eventually became the partner of Mrs. Meek in whippet affairs, sharing the Chancerick affix. Mrs. Griffith and her husband subsequently retired to Wales and the younger whippets are rotated between them, Mrs. Meek training them for racing, showing and coursing, which is followed by a country holiday for the dogs. The older dogs either visit or live permanently with one or the other and this arrangement works excellently, the whippets settling happily in either home, all living in the house.

Chisige Ricky was sired by Shalfleet Shimmer, who was litter brother to Shalfleet Saga and although there were no pedigree whippet racing clubs at that time, Ricky had his share of wins and qualified and ran at the first B.W.R.A. Championships at Wetherby. Mrs. Meek also became interested in showing but began to accumulate whippets, and when pedigree clubs began to form she returned to racing in order to prove that their dogs could do as well on the track as in the ring.

In the first season of the East Anglian Whippet Coursing Club 1971/2, Chancerick Nimrodel Rosefinch (Ch. Poltesco Peewit ex

Nimrodel Wintersweet), racing name Rupoo, was top bitch on points, and was mated to the dog who was joint top dog on points, Ebzan Noudini Bey Noir (Kalo) who is by Ch. Ladiesfield Bedazzled out of Fleeting Fashion Plate.

Barbara Griffith and Hilda Meek share the opinion that if a whippet is made to the Kennel Club standard and can win in the show ring, it should be able to win on the track and in the field. Rupoo and Kalo are both winners in the show ring; Rupoo is litter sister to Ch. Nimrodel Ruff. From their first litter came Chancerick Koh-i-Noor (Koko), Chancerick Kala (Velvet), Chancerick Kondor, Chancerick Kismet, Chancerick Khiva, Chancerick Kaspar and Chancerick Kaloson. Koko, Velvet and Kondor are Whippet Club Racing Champions; Kismet had a very bad shoulder injury at two years old but has won a lot of races. Koko, Velvet, Kismet, Kasper and Kaloson have all done well in the show ring and have been shown at Crufts Dog Show; Kasper has won one Challenge Certificate and one Reserve C.C.; Khiva has won in the ring and at coursing; Kaloson, in the East Anglian Whippet Coursing Club, was top dog puppy on points in 1973/4 and has been top adult dog for three years in succession.

At four years old, Koko has already sired over 100 puppies to show, racing and coursing bitches and his progeny are winning on the track, in the ring and in the field.

LAGUNA KENNELS

Established in 1939 by Mrs. D. U. McKay of Newbury, Berkshire. From her first whippet, Tiptree Joan, Mrs. McKay bred her first Show Champions with two bitches from this litter. Jovial Judy from the same litter brought the first Champion Dog, Ch. Laguna Liege, winner of seven C.C.s including Best in Show at the Whippet Club Jubilee Show. Liege was the sire of American Ch. Laguna Lucky Lad out of Ch. Brekin Ballet Shoes, outstanding for his award for the first whippet ever to have won the Hound Group at the Great Westminster All Breed Championship Show in the U.S.A. Liege's progeny also included Ch. Laguna Lullaby, a very successful northern winner.

The lovely bitch Brekin Ballet Shoes was acquired, gaining her title in 1953, and out of a daughter of hers, Laguna Lilibet, came the blue brindle dog International Ch. Laguna Libretto, who made a big name on the Continent, winning, with many other awards, Best in Show All Breeds at the Brussels International Championship Show 1953. Ch. Brekin Ballet Shoes was the dam of Champions Limelight and Lily of Laguna, dual winners of the Dog and Bitch C.C.s at Leeds Championship Show under Mrs. Garrish. Ballet Shoes was also the dam of the world-famous Ch. Laguna Ligonier—eight C.C.s and sire of eleven English Champions, an all-time record (for those times), also innumerable International and European Champions including the well-known American Ch. Greenbrae Barn Dance—a multi-Best in Show winner and all-time top producing winner in America.

Ligonier's full sister Ch. Laguna Leading Lady was dam of litter Champions Laguna Linkway and Lucia (dam of Barn Dance) who were dual winners of the Dog and Bitch C.C.s at the Three Counties Championship Show, Linkway, winning Best of Breed and Best in Show All Breeds.

Ch. Laguna Limelight is sire of the successful International Champion Laguna Locomite (dam Ch. Laguna Leading Lady) which started Bo Bengtson towards his path of fame in the Whippet World of Sweden. Bo later acquired a son of Ligonier, Laguna Leader, soon making him into an International Champion and whose pedigree lines feature in most of the top winners of today.

Ch. Laguna Light Lagoon, grandson of Limelight, is chiefly noted for his outstanding progeny of successful coursing and racing stock, he is also sire of Canadian Ch. Laguna Leo, one of the top ten Sighthounds Obedience winners.

Laguna Lamplighter, owned by the Duchess of Devonshire, was a regular 'member' of the shooting parties and worked with the retrieving dogs with great success.

Since the Whippet Coursing Club was founded in 1963, the

majority of Mrs. McKay's whippets have enjoyed regular organised coursing. Some of Lagoon's outstanding winners in the coursing field were Madison Moonlake, winner of the Open Dog Stakes at the Alderton Finals for three consecutive years; Laguna Lacquer, top stake winning dog for two consecutive seasons of the Whippet Coursing Club and sire of Papedaro Black Prince, winner of the Woolley Cup. Other winners in the coursing field include Laguna Lintino, Silver Shadow, Silver Sadie, Fairfold Fancy of Laguna, Laguna Lennox and Lirico of Laguna.

Dorrit McKay's first introduction to whippet racing was during the war year of 1943 whilst living in Lancashire, with her original whippet Tiptree Joan. On Sunday afternoons quite a few whippet enthusiasts would gather in a field and dogs would race on a yard per pound system with hand-operated traps and the inevitable bicycle wheel lure. When she moved south again, whippet racing had not caught on, nor was the breed very popular around her district until the 1960s when Mrs. McKay and some whippeteer friends organised fortnightly meetings at Padworth, near Reading, the home of Mrs. Josephine Creasy, world-famous All Breed judge who most kindly offered one of her paddocks for a racetrack.

One of the keenest contestants was Ligonier, but the most outstanding dog from the 'Laguna' kennels was Limelight, rather a large (for those days) silver fawn who also proved himself one of the top coursing dogs of that period. Limelight passed on his racing genes to many of his progeny, the best-known nowadays being his grandson Ch. Laguna Light Lagoon who, although never participating in organised racing or coursing himself, sired many well-known racing and coursing whippets including W.C.R.A. Ch. Laguna Lintino (Shadow), Madison Moonlake (Luke) and Lirico of Laguna (Kipper), winner of the East of England Coursing Club 1976 Puppy Stakes and the Oxford W.R.C. Sparky Challenge Trophy.

Ligonier's son Laguna Liberty Lad, winner of two C.C.s and keener on the sport than the show ring, proved a consistent winner in the sixties and is sire of Laguna Lilywhite (Snow) who in turn sired W.C.R.A. Ch. Laguna Lolita (Tessa) and W.C.R.A. Ch. Laguna Lauraine (Candy), dam of W.C.R.A. Ch. Laguna Linneth (Mitzie).

CULVERSTREET WHIPPETS

Group Captain Harry and Mrs. 'Freddie' Whittingham breed high quality whippets at a medieval manor-house near Burford, Oxford. Their object is to breed whippets capable of winning at racing and coursing, which may also show well, and they use a few outstanding bitches who have proved themselves on the track and in the coursing field. Breeding is for even temperament, intelligence, determination, speed and stamina.

W.C.R.A. Ch. Laguna Lauraine (Candy)

Sire Laguna Lilywhite, dam Laguna Lauretta, whelped 21 May 1969, weight 22 lb, height 18 inches, bred by Mrs. D. U. McKay. She became W.C.R.A. 22-lb. Champion, and during her career won many honours at the Oxford Whippet Racing Club and found fame with the Whippet Coursing Club and Woolley Coursing Club. Even at seven and a half years old, she won the Woolley Coursing Club Landowners' Nomination Stake (mixed).

By Ch. Laguna Light Lagoon she produced W.C.R.A. Ch. Laguna Linneth, 18-lb. Champion.

By W.C.R.A. Ch. Chancerick Koh-i-Noor (Koko) she produced Culverstreet Cherry (Lucky) 30-lb weight class winner. Litter sister Culverstreet Chianti has proved very successful in both racing and coursing and little brother Culverstreet Courvoisier, a blue, has made his mark in the show ring.

Laguna Luisa (Clover)

Sire Laguna Lilywhite, dam Laguna Great Circle Marjorie, whelped 17 October 1969, bred by Mrs. D. U. McKay. This

23-lb., 18½-inch bitch was an exceptional coursing whippet having won twelve stakes from the age of sixteen months when she took the Whippet Coursing Club Invitation Stakes at Sedgeford Manor, Norfolk, beating her father in the semi-final. Win followed win in the coursing field and she was still in the limelight even as a veteran. Success also came her way at the Oxford W.R.C.

W.C.R.A. CH. LAGUNA LINTINO (SHADOW)

Sire Ch. Laguna Light Lagoon, dam Laguna Great Circle Marjorie, whelped 11 October 1972, weight 20 lb., height 17½ inches, bred by Mrs. D. U. McKay. She was W.C.R.A. Champion (20 lb.) and notched up successes at Oxford W.R.C. At the Woolley Whippet Coursing Club she divided the Open Puppy Stakes, the Rookery Farm Stakes and won the Upthorpe Stakes and the Whitleather Lodge Trophy. She was runner-up in the Woolley Cup in March 1975 to Papedaro Black Prince. In October 1976 she won the Woolley Club Church Farm Stakes (mixed) beating the 1976 Woolley Cup winner I'm Quickest in the final. I'm Quickest had beaten the 1975 Woolley Cup winner Papedaro Black Prince in the first round, which was a remarkable achievement by such a small whippet.

CASALOMA WHIPPETS

Mrs. Clare England of Downton, near Salisbury, Wiltshire acquired her first whippet, a fawn bitch named Fleet, weighing 22 lb. and began racing her at eighteen months at the New Forest Whippet Racing Club. The bitch showed up well on the track, beating some of the best dogs in the south. She also raced at Weymouth Open (greyhound track) and won the 24-lb. class.

At five years old, Fleet had her first litter to the late Jim Cordell's Son of Sid, a very well-known dog in the south and, from this litter, came R. Ch. Sailor, a very handsome brindle dog owned by Mrs. Margaret Baker of Camberley. Later, Sailor (registered name Casaloma Misty Morn) was mated to Casaloma Shanie, a 24-lb. brindle bitch who raced well as a youngster, and from this litter came Casaloma Cobber, a 26-lb. brindle who became a W.C.R.A. Champion before he was two years old, also Casaloma Coronet (racing name Matelot), 24 lb., a very useful open racer.

Another bitch owned by Mrs. England is Selbrook Siona (Karla)—not related to Fleet—and she was mated to Knockaphrumpa, producing Beetle (Casaloma Cassandra) and litter sister Renée (Casaloma Coral). Beetle became a Racing Champion in 1976 in the 16-lb. class and has done very well in club racing at the Andover and Surrey Clubs, also reaching ten open finals in 1976. Renée has also featured in open finals and was mated to R.Ch. Our Pepe, the litter including Mrs. England's 22-lb. bitch My Beauty, who has proved her worth at the Andover Club.

MARTINSELL WHIPPETS

The Martinsell affix is shared by Mrs. Joanna Russell and Mrs. Caroline Brown, who bought as their foundation dogs Ladiesfield Dazzling (bred by Mrs. Wigg by Ch. Ladiesfield Bedazzled ex Ladiesfield Black Shadow) and Shalfleet Saga (bred by Mrs. B. Wilton-Clark by Porthurst Cherry Brandy ex Wingedfoot Bartette). Both dogs sired a number of Martinsell litters and are behind many of today's racing winners. Saga was a particularly outstanding sire, although not a very fast dog himself. Among his offspring are W.C.R.A. Ch. Kimberley, owned by Mr. Pickett, and W.C.R.A. Ch. Vangirl, owned by Mrs. Keable. He also sired W.C.R.A. finalists Martinsell Firethorn (Whisper), Martinsell Miranda, Martinsell Marsh Mallow (Ben Haze), Silvercreek Snow Queen and Simon D. He is grandsire of W.C.R.A. Ch. Valentine's Link, Karen's Lad, Firethorn, W.C.R.A. Ch. Picketty Witch, W.C.R.A. Ch. Fulmen Firefly (Miss Twitty), Fulmen French Fern (Ripple) and White Lady.

Mrs. Watts's Fulmen litter was sired by Shalfleet Schelle out of

Silver Creek Snow Queen. Kimberley, Vangirl, Valentine's Link and Rose of Firethorn were all out of the same bitch, April Rose, owned by Mr. Casson of Abbotts Ann.

Saga sired not only racing winners, but show winners as well, including Dutch Champion Longrove Larkspur, Martinsell Passion Flower and Martinsell Snapdragon, the latter being behind several of today's show and racing winners. Shalfleet Saga died in 1973 of a heart condition, but his bloodlines continue to produce excellent racers.

SPOKES WHIPPETS

The first introduction to these 'fragile' dogs for Mr. and Mrs. P. Spokes was a blue pup out of Nimrodel Bilberry of Allways out of Garden Party of Allways. Named Nimrodel Shot Silver (Jake) this good-natured dog quickly established himself as a great pet and slept on his owners' bed until his unfortunate death as a result of a road accident. Meanwhile, when Jake was four years old the Spokes took a three-month-old rescue bitch and registered it as Dawn's Pride. Later she was mated with Mrs. McKay's Laguna Lacquer to produce the Woolley Cup winner of 1974/5, Papedaro Black Prince.

It wasn't long before the couple were bitten by the racing bug, visiting Brackley on several occasions, but wanting very much to start their own club. They achieved this when, together with four or five other whippet owners, they began racing at Kidlington and this was the start of Oxford Club. One thing led to another and it wasn't long before Peter and Pamela Spokes were involved with the Whippet Club Racing Association, organising Championship meetings and so on.

The next successful whippet at the Spokes Kennels was Karyannup Striker (Laguna Lacquer ex Karyannup Suzanna The Lady) who won the 20-lb. class in the autumn of 1972 at the Surrey track and has since been dogged with toe injuries, inconvenient seasons and other misfortunes and consequently that vital second Championship win—and therefore the title of Racing Champion—has eluded her.

The latest acquisitions are Karyon Kalypso and Karyon Kuilla, being second and third matings of Abbotts Anny Pride (Shy Boy) out of W.C.R.A. Ch. Vangirl, which produced the great open racer W.C.R.A. Ch. Picketty Witch.

WARD WHIPPETS

W.C.R.A. Champion Lucky Venture, whelped March 1970, has been a top-class racing whippet. Her normal racing weight is $21\frac{1}{2}$ lb. and she runs all her races with terrific determination, and also has outstanding ability for bend racing. This white and fawn bitch began her racing career with the New Forest W.R.C. at the age of eleven months, winning her first major trophy seven months later. Success also came her way in W.C.R.A. Championship racing, where she won the two classes necessary for a Champion title. With over 200 wins to her credit, she produced her first litter (by W.C.R.A. Ch. Jack's Boy) in September 1976.

Another charge of the Ward Kennels in Tidworth, Hampshire, is the 20-lb. black and white bitch Cloudy Venture who, although unpredictable, has been a good club racing whippet.

FIELD WHIPPETS

The notable racing dogs owned by Muriel and Harry Field began with Caroles Penny Black, first raced with the Welwyn W.R.C. and proving to be a very consistent, successful little bitch, racing weight 20 lb.

Her two daughters, Caroles Black Ranee and Caroles Honey Lass, were sired by the Fields' own blue dog Caroles Blue Peter; these were two of the fastest pedigree bitches of their day. Black Ranee ran second to the great Racing Champion Snowflake in the first ever B.W.R.A. National Finals at Wetherby in what was a

D   93

close decision. Both she and her sister were club champions of the Welwyn and Stanborough Clubs, both weighing 22 lb.

The latest racing bitches from the Field Kennels are Caroles Blue Zelda (better known as Racing Champion Peanut) and Caroles Blue Tuana, both out of Black Ranee by Racing Champion Our Pepe. R. Ch. Peanut has won five W.C.R.A. National Finals, spanning two weight groups, 20 lb. and 22 lb., also a number of pedigree opens. Her sister Blue Tuana, although a strong, fast, 26-lb. bitch and a finalist on a number of occasions, seemed prone to bad luck, clocking up more than her fair share of injuries.

This spans about twelve years' racing with above average results with about 250 cups, trophies, etc., and two Championship jackets.

FULMEN WHIPPETS

Silver Creek Snow Queen (Shalfleet Saga ex Martinsell Mignonette) is owned by Mrs. N. J. Watts and is winner of one Championship, having gained runner-up placing on two other occasions. One of her outstanding performances was at the July 1973 Championships held at Surrey when her time of 15·75 in an under 23-lb. heat was only bettered by 0·05 in a 30-lb race. Her time of 15·84 was the fastest time recorded for any final that day. Another occasion when she excelled herself was at the Oxford open in September of the same year when she clocked times of 15·90 twice and 16·19 in the semi-final, before winning the final in 16·19 after two re-runs. She has produced two outstanding daughters (sire Shalfleet Schelle) in Fulmen Firefly (Miss Twitty) and Fulmen French Fern (Ripple), the former winning her two Championships in 1973 and many trophies, while the latter was one-time track record holder at Surrey but always managed to become injured (or had found the 'Purina' sack during the week before a Championship!)

A grandson of Snow Queen, Martinsell Molasses (Oliver Twist) won his first Championship in July 1974 and two more in 1975.

94

His sire is the unraced Fulmen Firecracker, litter brother to Miss Twitty and Ripple.

OTHER NOTABLE PEDIGREES

PICKETTY WITCH

One of the most outstanding pedigree racing whippets, this black and white bitch was whelped in October 1973 out of Mrs. Joyce Keable's W.C.R.A. Champion Vangirl, sired by R. Casson's Abbots Anny Pride (Shy Boy). Weighing 23 lb., her pedigree name is Karyon Sootican Princess and her owner, Terry Peart, races her at Andover and Oxford Clubs when not busy on the Open circuit.

Out of seven W.C.R.A. Championships entered in succession, no less than seven victories have been achieved by this remarkable animal, winning every qualifying race except one, which was second place in a re-run heat. Her open wins are many and she has numerous club trophy wins to her credit. From her first 165 races, she has gained 117 wins, 39 second placings and 9 other placings.

RUSSETTWOOD PAGEANT

This son of Ch. Laguna Ligonier was a winner of Firsts at Championship and Open shows, Best Hound, Best Sporting, etc., also Firsts at Racing and Obedience. He is well known as being the sire of Mystic Pepe (Our Pepe—Racing Champion in B.W.R.A. and W.C.R.A. Championships), also Patch of Bemerton (Jimpy), Woolmer Wayfarer (Jake), Chilworth Pride (Chilworth Girl), Balley Will Will (Little Mo), Lucky Venture—all W.C.R.A. Champions. When mated to the greyhound bitch Sarah, the result was B.W.R.A. Champions Melvina B and Mary Mint.

Russettwood Pageant also sired Ricardo Roulette who produced W.C.R.A. Ch. Our Kid, Our Pest and Our Lisa; his litter sister show champion Russettwood Portia (9 C.C.s) produced to Ch. L. Linkway W.C.R.A. Ch. Russettwood Moonshine, winner three times in succession.

Chapter Thirteen

CHOOSING A PUP

Big, small, tall, short, longbacked, stocky—top-class racing whippets may fall under any of these categories, so how can one possibly choose a puppy from a litter of, say, six healthy youngsters?

Newcomers to the sport may take some comfort from the fact that even the most experienced whippeteer chooses with great deliberation and then may come off with the poorest in the litter. Owing to demand for pups from well-known parents, the choice has to be made very early, often even the day of birth, so obviously it is impossible to knowingly choose the best. At a mere two or three weeks old, with the odd exception, it is hard to tell to what size the dogs will grow; often the biggest in the litter at birth may eventually be overtaken in size by its littermates. Some people like certain colours; some like the pup with the longest tail; others go for a certain order of whelping (i.e. first born, second born); a pup which is a demanding feeder and bulldozes the others out of the way to satisfy its appetite also commands attention, as does a forward pup who peers cutely at a prospective buyer.

Whatever your fancy, though, it all boils down to a game of chance; in fact, I have known the most enlightened of whippet-owners who, when picking a pup, merely shut their eyes and take the first touched! If, however, a buyer selects a well-bred litter, the chances of a future open racer are quite good.

BREEDING COUNTS

The secret of acquiring a decent racer lies in choosing the right parents in the first place. This is a little easier for someone who has been in the sport for a time but, to a beginner, the choice is bewildering. How does he know that pups out of one racing champion should be better than those from another who has gained similar honours?

One way to heighten the chances of getting a future champion is to go for a pup from a proven mating, i.e. a repeat of a litter which has proved its worth at open race level. Plenty of such pups are available but, understandably, these are in great demand, so it is advisable to book your pup well in advance, even before the bitch is in pup if a previous litter has been outstanding. Offspring from proven matings tend to be highly priced but, at best, an open whippet will be the reward and, at worst, a good club dog should result.

It does not automatically follow that a pup from an open-class bitch will itself be a winner, but the chances increase if the dam also has brothers and sisters who show great aptitude on the racetrack. In other words, consistency is the keyword in whippet breeding. A bitch whose dam was a good sort and who herself is from a good litter should, if mated to a sire whose record is equally impressive, produce good-quality racing pups. Once again, prices tend to be higher but this can be cheaper in the long run.

There are many good sires advertising their services and all possess good racing bloodlines, but the bitch must be a decent brood or mediocre pups will result whichever dog sires the litter. Good brood bitches, as a rule, tend to have been lightly raced and are usually of a decent size.

Don't be misled into buying a pup purely because the dam was a real flying machine—study the bitch, as one of strong build is more desirable; study also the rest of her litter for, if she was the only one to perform well, the chances are lower of pups possessing that vital spark. Before buying, a k about the running ability of grandparents, aunts, uncles, etc., particularly on the dam's side.

LOWLIER BACKGROUNDS

Not all open racers, by any means, come from famous parents; indeed, many hail from much more modest backgrounds. A bitch who, although not a winner at open level, has shown herself to be a backmarker in club racing, is very often, if mated to a decent sire, responsible for an extremely good litter. Here again, preferably she should have been fairly lightly raced (some owners race their dogs as many as three or four times a week in summer). Evidence that brothers and sisters are also of reasonable quality points to the possibility of good offspring. Pups from this type of litter can be expected to be reasonably priced, and also, a buyer has more reason to be smug if his hunch pays off!

Often it happens that a bitch who is not too fast herself but whose brothers and sisters are open or good class, produces better pups than her more famous sisters. Because she carries the same blood as her faster littermates, even though she did not make the grade on the track, chances are high of a good litter, especially as she has probably not been raced as heavily as her open class sisters. So don't be put off if she was the slowest in the litter—the blood is there and has every chance of materialising into a winner. By purchasing one from such a litter, a good racer at a bargain price can be the result.

If a dam has never been up to much at club level, nor have any of her litter or close relatives, it is unlikely that any of her progeny will do great things. But there are enthusiasts whose interest lies purely in club handicaps and such a person would find this type of pup quite adequate; it is pointless paying big money for a whippet if it is only required for club racing.

GREYHOUND BLOOD

A lot of breeding is also carried out by putting small greyhound bitches to lightweight whippet dogs. This has been rewarded with quite a measure of success, but prospective buyers should think carefully before purchasing. Most clubs operate on the ruling that dogs should be 'smooth-haired and whippet-like in appearance' (offspring come into this category) but many, including the British Whippet Racing Association, also enforce a strict 32-lb. weight limit. While lots of the youngsters resulting from these greyhound/whippet unions come within the weight limit, many exceed it, and an owner can be bitterly disappointed if his hopes of running the dog are frustrated because of size. There are a few notable brood bitches among the greyhounds which have thrown excellent racing stock eligible to run on whippet tracks but, alas, I fear that many have jumped on to the bandwagon and some indiscriminate breeding takes place. If this type of pup is desired, tread carefully, particularly if choosing a dog pup, and be prepared that it might go over the top!

READYMADE RACER

One way to make sure of an open racer is to buy an older whippet. Not many are available as, understandably, it is the aim of most whippeteers to own an open race dog. Sometimes circumstances force the sale of a good-class racer, but expect to pay into three figures for such a dog. Make sure, when making this type of purchase, that the reason for the sale is genuine and there is no underlying reason for the dog being sold.

Chapter Fourteen

REARING A PUP

Many owners prefer to take possession of racing pups as young as six weeks old; this is contrary to a lot of other breeds where eight weeks is more common for leaving the dam.

Before accepting a puppy, make sure it is independent of the bitch, being completely weaned. Worming should also have been attended to, although it is possible that a pup may have been wormed once and the new owner will be required to give the second dose when due. Ascertain which type of worming agent was used; the breeder may supply the correct dosage for the new owner to administer.

Ideally, dew claws should have been removed, as this is a simple matter when pups are a few days old, but entails anaesthetising the animal if the operation has to be performed later in the dog's life. As painful injury can occur during racing by dew claws being caught in the dog's muzzle, etc., most whippet-owners agree that removal of dew claws a few days after birth is the best policy.

It is desirable that someone should be at home during the day to see the pup has adequate meals, as young dogs require regular feeding. At first, four meals a day should be provided, two being milk foods such as powdered babymilk (Ostermilk Two is recommended; simply mix a little powder with hot water, mix to a paste, then add cold water), alternatively there are equivalent products on the canine market. Cows' milk is unsuitable as the protein percentage is too low for growing pups and, although goats' milk has a slightly higher protein percentage, this is not very suitable either. Powdered baby cereal (Farex, etc.) is also very good in the early days, and an occasional saucerful of porridge will make a youngster thrive. A little raw egg mixed with one of the milk meals three or four days a week will be appreciated as this is a good source of calcium; another daily addition should be a quarter-teaspoonful of bonemeal, which is another source of calcium.

The two other meals should consist of meat or fish; minced raw or cooked meat, tinned meat, rabbit, chicken, white fish, tinned sardines or pilchards, kippers or a well-boiled sheep's head (remove the bones)—all are excellent for a growing whippet. If variety can be offered, then all the better. Once a week a small amount of raw or lightly boiled liver may be given. Add to the meal a good teaspoonful of junior baby food also (the type available in small glass jars), which is a mixture of meat or chicken and vegetables and is readily prepared and very convenient. Mix with the meat or fish a small handful of puppy meal (available from pet shops, or ordinary dog meal crushed small serves just as well). The dog meal should not be soaked, as teeth also need to be kept healthy! Brown bread, dried in the oven, also serves well in place of meal. Fresh water should be available at all times.

By twelve weeks, right up to six months, three meals a day are sufficient, the quantity being increased proportionately according to growth. The morning meal should still consist of babymilk, but breakfast cereal should now be added in the place of the powdered version and, on alternate days, mix some beaten raw egg with the milk, leaving out the cereal. Continue with one quarter of a teaspoonful of bonemeal once a day, sprinkled on the morning meal. The remaining meals should still be of meat or fish, dry biscuits and vegetables, but increase the amount as the pup grows.

A lot is talked about vitamins, and many people add these in the form of pills, powders, etc., but really, a dog should get most of these from its food. The secret is to give a whippet a varied diet. This way it gets all the vitamins it needs in its food. Don't overcook meat or vegetables, as those precious vitamins may be destroyed, and add also some of the water in which the meat or vegetables have been cooked. If a pup is being fed as suggested above, then it will be getting all the essential vitamins, provided all the products are fresh (make sure baby products are not out of date as vitamins may have deteriorated).

A cod liver oil capsule may be given daily (don't give capsules which have been stored in the cupboard a long time, buy a fresh pack). Alternatively, a few drops of cod liver oil liquid can be given (about four or five drops only); here again, this has a short storage life and, ideally, should be kept in a refrigerator.

The main item a pup needs is calcium, and this can be ensured by feeding babymilk, baby cereal, eggs, bread and bonemeal.

Chapter Fifteen

PUPPY TRAINING

About the age of three months, providing the weather is right, a pup should be introduced to the racetrack, the idea being to accustom him to the noise as early as possible. An ideal spot to stand with a pup is behind the trapman, this usually being the noisiest place on the track. He will soon associate the noise of the traps as a signal for his elders to show their paces and, being very quick to learn, it will not take him long to start straining at the leash, as after all, it is his natural instinct to want to run and chase.

When he is unaffected by all the sounds around him, he should be brought to the side of the traps to enable him to see the lure, thus conveying to him what the whippets are chasing after. To get him more interested the owner could wave a piece of cloth close to the ground (not in the pup's face) but far enough in front of him so he is not scared. A child is an ideal ploy for this, as both the pup and child think it is great fun.

This can also be utilised when training the pup to enter the traps. It is no good placing a pup in a trap and expecting him to come out chasing straight away. If he is held in the trap from behind with the trap front up, and let through a few times to the rag-waving child, he will not be too disturbed when the trap front is closed.

This is the time when the lure should be placed in front of him, and taken slowly away from the trap, so he can see it properly;

15 to 20 yards is ample distance at this stage of training. By this time the pup should be four and a half to five months old and beginning to look like a racing whippet. The distance he runs from the trap should be extended weekly, and in a few weeks he should be racing up to 100 yards.

It should be stressed at this point that the virtue is patience at all times, as some pups are much quicker to learn than others. When a pup has finally reached the 100-yard mark, it is time to see how he performs with other dogs. This is a crucial time for him, and the advice here is to find an old, honest dog, giving him a few yards' start, but likely to catch him. You will soon find whether he has any vices in him by the way he reacts when another dog is by his side. Many pups have been spoiled by being thrown in at the deep end and their owners hoping for the best; it is far better to lose a few weeks' training than to have him spoiled by being tackled, bumped or interfered with by other pups wanting to play.

After three or four times with one dog against him he should be ready to start his racing career. On the whole, it takes a bitch nine months and a dog twelve months to start to show its true racing ability, but obviously there are exceptions to the rule.

As to getting a pup used to wearing a muzzle, simply training him in a muzzle should suffice; don't muzzle the pup, then leave him for a long period wearing it, as the dog may develop a hatred of the muzzle and problems may arise in that the dog will try to remove the muzzle in the trap.

Chapter Sixteen

ADULT TRAINING AND FEEDING

By the time a bitch is nine months or a dog twelve months, an owner must start training the dog to get him to peak fitness. Individuals have their own ideas on this subject, but experience has found that a one- to two-mile walk on the road, first thing in the morning, and a two-mile walk in the evening, plus a few minutes off the lead for a scamper round, is sufficient to keep a whippet in good condition. Walks should be varied as much as possible for, like human beings, dogs appreciate a change in their surroundings.

After each period of exercise the dog's feet should be washed in Dettol or something similar to ensure there are no small stones and so on in his pads. Also, inspect the eyes for bits of grass, etc. Another important aspect for the benefit of a racing dog is grooming, which is a 'must' if a dog is to be kept looking tiptop. A 'dandy' brush is ideal for loosening any mud on the dog's coat and, being stiff, this acts as a comb also. A rubber-spiked brush is another essential as this gives a massaging effect. Follow these with a hound glove and an owner will be delighted with the results of this daily chore.

Now we come to the other vital part of keeping a dog in racing condition, that of feeding. Once again, individuals have their own ideas on this subject, and who can argue if they are getting results?

It must be accepted that proteins, carbohydrates and fats are the three classifications of food necessary to a dog. Proteins build muscle and promote growth, while carbohydrates and fats create energy and heat. This is a simplified explanation of this important subject and gives a rough idea of the principles.

What are classified as proteins? They are meat, fish, eggs and milk. Carbohydrates are found in vegetables and cereals. Fats of any sort are found in meat, cod liver oil, milk, etc.

A dog is a carnivorous animal (meat eating) so a preference is for fresh meat against the modern trend to dried food. Watch a dog when he catches a rabbit, he will devour the lot if allowed, and this is his natural way of obtaining his balanced diet. There are many kinds of meat available and, as in training, variety is the spice of life. Liver, kidneys, hearts and so on should always be minced and well cooked. When mixed with cooked vegetables, meal, etc., the food should never be soggy. If a person insists upon feeding soaked dog biscuits with the meal (in my opinion, biscuits should be fed dry) then these should be soaked in cold water, as hot water tends to draw out the vitamin contents. Raw tripe is another good food for a dog and this may be fed as a main meal once a week.

A typical day's diet would be:

BREAKFAST: Half a pint of tepid milk with beaten egg (alternate daily, with half a pint of tepid milk and cereal).

MAIN MEAL: One pound of minced meat mixed with dog meal, also vegetables (carrot, parsnips, cabbage, turnip tops, etc.). Vary daily, i.e. rabbit, oxtail, liver, fish, etc.

One teaspoonful of cod liver oil about three times per week during winter months—not as important in summer. One teaspoonful of seaweed powder each day supplements any vitamins which may be missing in the dog's diet.

In days gone by, when whippet meetings were few and far between, a dog was specially trained and prepared for a specific race meeting; nowadays, dogs are running once, twice or even three times a week, therefore the secret is simply to keep the animal fit and, following this feeding and training method, an owner will not go far wrong.

A bitch whippet who has seasons at regular intervals will, if kept exercised and correctly fed, run with consistency until just prior to coming in season, when her performance will usually improve up to her actually springing.

This is another subject upon which ideas are divided—that of whether or not a bitch should be raced after a season. During the three weeks the bitch is actually on heat she should not be raced because, although not actually harming her, it is very antisocial and causes havoc amongst the male competitors, who cannot be expected to put their hearts into the racing when they can smell a bitch in season! When the bitch is off heat, there is no reason why she cannot be raced for about four weeks, except that she may still be carrying a scent and distract the dogs. A bitch should be rested from the sixth to about the tenth week from first coming into season. Occasionally, a bitch may come into milk even though a mating has not taken place—watch carefully for this, as mastitis could result if she were raced. I would favour resting a bitch for the full twelve weeks, from first coming into season, ensuring she has a good rest and is raring to go once more when the time is right. A bitch loses yards after being in season but, by twelve weeks from the first day, she will be beginning to show her old potential and, by sixteen weeks, all her old verve should be back! Her form then should be consistent until her next season.

Bitches tend to put on a little weight during a seasonal rest; keep an eye on this and, if she is overweight, increase her roadwork for a week or two to get her back to racing weight.

Although a dog whippet does not, of course, have seasons, he cannot be expected to give good performances indefinitely. A few weeks' rest will be appreciated from time to time, and bring the dog back bouncing! The best way is to check the racing calendar and plan the resting period accordingly. Still give the dog a daily walk as he enjoys this, and it will prevent him piling on weight. The beauty of racing dog whippets is that an owner may

choose the dog's resting period as opposed to the enforced resting
of bitches.

TACKLERS

Occasionally the problem arises of a dog which 'tackles' another
dog or plays about during a race. This will more than likely get the
dog disqualified from the race and, if he persists, will get the dog
barred from the club until he ceases this practice. Causes of this
are varied: wrong training tactics, being allowed too much
freedom off the lead, or the problem could be bred into the dog.
Many 'cures' have been tried with varying degrees of success,
depending on the dog.

One thing is certain, a dog learning its job must not be allowed
to run about freely with other whippets because he will then
associate racing with just another jolly game! If he has free
exercise, this must be strictly alone where no other dogs can
interfere.

Follow the training procedure given in this book and, if the dog
persists in playing about, the first thing to do is lay him off racing,
as no purpose will be served by continuing to run him. Give the
dog plenty of solo lurework, allowing him to catch the lure and
build up his keenness. If he still seems indifferent to the lure, try
luring him with an onion sack with a morsel of meat inside which
should be fed to the dog at the end of the race. Gradually re-
introduce him to other participants by running just one honest
dog with him, allowing the dog to be overtaken and continue to
'reward' him each time.

Most dogs will grow out of this 'tackling' phase but, of course,
some are never cured, which is a great pity. For the more serious
'offenders' more drastic measures may be tried; for instance,
blinkers fixed to the muzzle often cure the problem so well that
eventually the blinkers may be dispensed with. Another method
which has been seen to work to a certain extent is to run the dog
from the back of the handicap, although in theory this shouldn't

work, as the dog can't see the lure too well from the back which, after all, is the whole object of the operation! One method which I am assured has a high success rate is to take the 'naughty' whippet together with a tried and trusted dog. Hold both dogs, each on a leash, with both leads in one hand. Get a colleague to very slowly pull an onion bag (or better still wind a hand lure) in front of the dogs, who will strain to reach it; when the dog inevitably turns on its partner, then tap him very firmly with a rolled-up newspaper. If this is carried out often enough, a dog may eventually learn not to turn his head.

In the event of all methods failing, give the dog a good long layoff, then start him at the very beginning once more; but the odd few can never be completely cured!

Chapter Seventeen

THE RISK OF INJURY

Whippet racing, of course, carries with it a risk of injury, but by observation of certain standards by clubs and owners, accidents and racing-associated illnesses can be kept to a minimum.

At any given race meeting there is always the risk of a collision should a dog not involved in the race break loose and run on to the track. Clubs are all too aware of this and most impose fines on the owners of any dog which runs loose, whether or not it interferes with runners. For their part, owners should be alert to this problem at all times, keeping a close eye on their charges; often the cause is a faulty collar or lead; here again, an owner should replace worn collars and leads as a matter of course. I have seen two top whippets—Missing Topaze and Jackson, both from Lancashire—killed by dogs running on to the track while a race is in progress!

Another cause of injury is when dogs collide at the finish, either with a pulley or with another participant. There are not many reports nowadays of collisions with equipment as clubs ensure this is as safe as possible and placed where it would be virtually impossible to cause an accident. A collision between two dogs sometimes can happen, more so when a dog wins by a great margin, and other dogs in the race then pile into the winner. However, whippets are extremely resilient, and injuries are infrequent in view of the amount of racing which takes place.

Owners should always take great care, when catching their dogs at the finish, to stand well back from the line—most clubs stipulate an area where handlers should stand. A dog travelling at 30 m.p.h. which runs into the legs of an owner can cause injury to itself and owner alike. Enthusiastic handlers have been known to move forward slowly but surely towards the line. This could be fatal and should be clamped down on very strongly. A rope across the width of the track, 25 yards over the line, is an effective barrier.

BEND INJURIES

Bend racing carries with it its own particular risks. N.G.A. greyhound tracks are now changing to outside hare because this system has been seen to be safer. However, whippets usually race at stadiums or training kennels where 'inside hare' is operated, and this can cause severe injuries should a dog be pushed into the rail. There is danger also to inexperienced dogs who jump the rail, which occurs quite often, and it is amazing that more dogs are not injured. Owners contemplating putting a dog on the bends should observe certain safety measures: (1) don't put a young or inexperienced whippet on the bends; (2) the first attempt for a dog who has never tried bend racing before should always be with a well-tried and trusted bend dog. If a dog is selected which shows similar capabilities on the straight, then the experienced dog will lead the newcomer round the bend track at a reasonable pace, so the new dog keeps sight of the lure and is not tempted to jump the rail; (3) don't be too impatient to run the dog in a bend handicap: make sure he is fully conversant with bend racing first.

Discussing the orthopaedic problems in the greyhound, Mr. P. R. Sweeney, Veterinary Surgeon, of Rugby, compares the risk of injury to a racing greyhound and that to a coursing animal. For over 6,000 years the greyhound proved its speed, skill and durability against wild hares on their own terrain, until it was set to chase the mechanical hare around an artificial course in 1926, when the now familiar pattern of injuries arose overnight.

The Risk of Injury

Although there is some risk of injury from the forces of acceleration in starting and of deceleration in stopping, the main problem seems to be caused by the conventional tracks, which consist of semicircular curves linking two straights. The gentle curve of the so-called first bend deceives the greyhound into a false sense of security; it careers headlong around to the second bend, where the vast majority of injuries are sustained.

To counteract centrifugal force, a dog must lean towards the inner fence; because of the extra load this thrusts on it, it is small wonder that instant or fatigue fractures of the carpal bones and ruptures of the flexor carpi ulnaris or triceps muscles or of the inner superficial flexor tendon are fairly common injuries.

Although the whippet is a smaller animal and therefore these dangers would occur to a lesser degree, owners should be aware of the extra risk attached to bend racing.

Chapter Eighteen

COMMON AILMENTS OF THE RACING WHIPPET

Because there are many excellent books on the subject of canine ailments, I do not propose to go into these except to highlight a few which are more common amongst racing whippets.

It is important that a dog has a full course of inoculations against distemper and hard pad, contagious hepatitis, leptospira canicola (*L. icterohaemorrhagiae*). Some clubs insist on vaccination certificates but most leave it to the conscience of the individual.

KENNEL COUGH

Kennel cough, or contagious respiratory disease, is highly infectious and once it gets a hold on the whippet fraternity it can cause havoc with race programmes. Ideally, any kennel contracting the disease should keep all dogs away from the track until well after all signs have cleared up. If an infected dog should attend a race meeting, then all dogs present risk getting the disease and passing it on to dogs in their own kennels. If the animal is rested and veterinary treatment sought in the more severe cases (one teaspoonful of glycerine mixed with one dessertspoonful of rosehip syrup gives relief in mild cases) a full recovery should result, but it is more dangerous to older dogs and

113

to young pups. A dog suffering from kennel cough should never be raced, even though, apart from a cough, the dog does not appear ill, and only irresponsible owners would even attempt to do so.

MANGE

Sarcoptic mange is caused by a mite burrowing into the superficial layers of the dog's skin where it lays its eggs and causes intense irritation.

The first sign is persistent scratching, usually followed by reddish patches in the armpits and insides of the thighs. It is possible to pass on this condition when dogs use collars or jackets provided by a club, and also by using the same starting boxes. One safeguard is for an owner to provide his own collars or jackets. Commercial products are available for treatment of mange, but a visit to the vet could save time and money in the long run. Bedding should be destroyed or disinfected.

FLEAS

Of course, where a large number of dogs are congregated, fleas are bound to be a nuisance from time to time. Shampoos, powders, combs, etc., are available to combat this problem, and bedding should be changed frequently. The common flea is prevalent in the summer and autumn, and it is important that dogs be kept free, as the flea is one of the intermediate hosts of the tapeworm.

FOOT AILMENTS

Care should be taken of a dog's stopper pads (found at the back of the forelegs, just below the knee) especially where the going is hard, as cuts and lacerations can happen when the dog uses these to absorb the shock when pulling up at the end of a race. If pads are cut, apply T.C.P. and cover until the wound dries up. Prevention is better than cure: tape up stoppers in hard going.

Cracked or peeling pads can occur and may cause lameness. Solution of permanganate of potash is a great standby for this kind of foot trouble (except where bleeding occurs); treat the condition daily. Alternatively, Padsanol is sold by greyhound and whippet suppliers and is good both for treatment of foot troubles and prevention of them.

While on the subject of feet, nails should be kept short, preferably by exercise, but if nails require trimming, care should be taken not to encroach on the quick or discomfort and possible bleeding will result.

KNOCKED-UP TOE

This is a fairly common injury, especially when the going is hard, and can be more serious when affecting toes of the fore-feet than the hind-feet.

It is wise to seek veterinary advice and possibly an x-ray to determine the whereabouts of the damage to the joint as, without correct care and attention, a hard fibrous body round the damaged joint can prevent the toe from moving when healed.

Chapter Nineteen

THE WHIPPET AS A PET

It is not necessary to take an interest in racing to enjoy the company of a whippet, for this little dog's affectionate nature and even temperament makes it an ideal pet.

One of its most attractive features is a smooth short coat, minimising the need for grooming, and the problems caused by dog hairs. An added bonus is that, as a general rule, a whippet does not like wet weather and will be disinclined to wade through puddles, then leave muddy footprints in the hall! A certain amount of exercise is appreciated by this breed, but not nearly so much as people imagine; a daily walk, or free exercise off the lead will keep him happy in spite of the fact that this animal adores the open spaces and a person who enjoys walking could choose no better companion. Basically, the whippet enjoys human company and whether that entails brisk walks, gambolling in the country-side, or being curled up at his master's feet matters little to this faithful animal.

No elaborate sleeping arrangements are required—a simple dog basket will suffice; a whippet isn't particular, so long as his bed is free from draughts. Being a medium- to small-sized dog, feeding costs are not horrific; this breed of dog is usually not too choosy about diet and any leftover table scraps (go easy on the potatoes!) can supplement his usual meat or fish and biscuits. Just a word of warning—beware of overfeeding purely because the animal

116

'looks thin'. A fat whippet looks grotesque, so care should be taken to keep the dog in trim. If the animal appears to be putting on too much weight, cut down on his food intake, particularly carbohydrates.

On the whole, whippets are intelligent creatures and will mould easily to their particular owner's requirements. In exchange for a good, careful upbringing and basic training, a whippet will be difficult to surpass as a faithful and game companion.

Chapter Twenty

MAKING CONTACT

Although whippet racing is enjoying ever increasing popularity, details of race meetings are not readily available unless a person resides in the locality of a whippet track. A list of track venues, and information regarding day and time of racing is available from P. Wilson, 3 Glebe Mount, Pudsey, West Yorkshire (Tel. Pudsey 572554). The national whippet magazine, *Whippet News*, is also published at this address and subscription rates are available upon request.